W9-BVM-452

BUILD YOUR OWN **KITCHEN CABINETS**

SECOND EDITION

DANNY PROULX

POPULAR
WOODWORKING
BOOKS

CINCINNATI, OHIO
www.popularwoodworking.com

The Joint Free Public Library
of
Morristown and Morris Township

read this important safety notice

To prevent accidents, keep safety in mind while you work. Use the safety guards installed on power equipment; they are for your protection. When working on power equipment, keep fingers away from saw blades, wear safety goggles to prevent injuries from flying wood chips and sawdust, wear headphones to protect your hearing, and consider installing a dust vacuum to reduce the amount of airborne sawdust in your woodshop. Don't wear loose clothing, such as neckties or shirts with loose sleeves, or jewelry, such as rings, necklaces or bracelets, when working on power equipment. Tie back long hair to prevent it from getting caught in your equipment. People who are sensitive to certain chemicals should check the chemical content of any product before using it. The authors and editors who compiled this book have tried to make the contents as accurate and correct as possible. Plans, illustrations, photographs and text have been carefully checked. All instructions, plans and projects should be carefully read, studied and understood before beginning construction. In some photos, power tool guards have been removed to more clearly show the operation being demonstrated. Always use all safety guards and attachments that come with your power tools. Due to the variability of local conditions, construction materials, skill levels, etc., neither the author nor Popular Woodworking Books assumes any responsibility for any accidents, injuries, damages or other losses incurred resulting from the material presented in this book. Prices listed for supplies and equipment were current at the time of publication and are subject to change. Glass shelving should have all edges polished and must be tempered. Untempered glass shelves may shatter and can cause serious bodily injury. Tempered shelves are very strong and if they break will just crumble, minimizing personal injury.

metric conversion chart

TO CONVERT	TO	MULTIPLY BY
Inches	Centimeters	2.54
Centimeters	Inches	0.4
Feet	Centimeters	30.5
Centimeters	Feet	0.03
Yards	Meters	0.9
Meters	Yards	1.1
Sq. Inches	Sq. Centimeters	6.45
Sq. Centimeters	Sq. Inches	0.16
Sq. Feet	Sq. Meters	0.09
Sq. Meters	Sq. Feet	10.8
Sq. Yards	Sq. Meters	0.8
Sq. Meters	Sq. Yards	1.2
Pounds	Kilograms	0.45
Kilograms	Pounds	2.2
Ounces	Grams	28.3
Grams	Ounces	0.035

Build Your Own Kitchen Cabinets, Second Edition. Copyright © 2003 by Danny Proulx. Manufactured in China. All rights reserved. No part of this book may be reproduced in any form or by any electronic or mechanical means including information storage and retrieval systems without permission in writing from the publisher, except by a reviewer, who may quote brief passages in a review. Published by Popular Woodworking Books, an imprint of F&W Publications, Inc., 4700 East Galbraith Road, Cincinnati, Ohio, 45236. First edition.

Visit our Web site at www.popularwoodworking.com for information on more resources for woodworkers.

Other fine Popular Woodworking Books are available from your local bookstore or direct from the publisher.

07   06   05   04   03   5   4   3   2   1

Library of Congress Cataloging-in-Publication Data

Proulx, Danny, 1947-
  Build your own kitchen cabinets / by Danny Proulx.-- 2nd ed.
     p. cm.
Includes index.
  ISBN 1-55870-676-3 (pbk. : alk. paper)
  1. Kitchen cabinets. 2. Cabinetwork. I. Title.
TT197.5.K57 P76 2003
684.1'6--dc21
                                2002152424

ACQUISITIONS EDITOR: Jim Stack
EDITOR: Jennifer Ziegler
DESIGNER: Brian Roeth
PRODUCTION COORDINATOR: Mark Griffin
PAGE LAYOUT ARTIST: Kathy Bergstrom
STEP-BY-STEP PHOTOGRAPHY BY: Danny Proulx
COVER AND CHAPTER LEAD PHOTOGRAPHY BY: Michael Bowie of Lux Photography
TECHNICAL ILLUSTRATIONS BY: Len Churchill
WORKSHOP SITE: Rideau Cabinets

Once again my "team" has come through to help me complete this book. Thanks to my wife, Gale, for her support and helping hand when needed, and to Jack Chaters, who is always ready to help. They are two important people.

Thanks also to Michael Bowie, who has been the primary photographer and photographic knowledge source for all my books. As a photographer and person, Michael is in a class of his own; he has a special gift.

The illustrations were revised and became works of art that were light-years in quality above the original drawings. Len Churchill is a talented illustrator with a unique style that few can match. Len is a real pleasure to work with and always gives more than requested.

The staff at Popular Woodworking Books is my support team, and I'm lucky to have such a talented and dedicated group of professionals. Editor Jim Stack and all the other talented and helpful members of the PW team are ready to help at a moment's notice. Thank you!

Thanks are also due to all the readers of my books who have sent pictures of completed projects, comments, suggestions and tips of their own for me to use. I truly appreciate your time and efforts.

about the author | Danny Proulx has been involved in the woodworking field for more than 30 years. He has operated a custom kitchen cabinet shop since 1989. Danny also teaches full-time and continuing-education students at Algonquin College in Ottawa, Ontario.

He is a contributing editor to *Cabinet-Maker* magazine and has published articles in other magazines such as *Canadian Home Workshop, Canadian Woodworking, Popular Woodworking, Woodshop News* and *Canadian Homes and Cottages*.

His earlier books include *The Kitchen Cabinetmaker's Building and Business Manual, How to Build Classic Garden Furniture, Smart Shelving & Storage Solutions, Fast & Easy Techniques for Building Modern Cabinetry, Building More Classic Garden Furniture, Building Cabinet Doors and Drawers, Build Your Own Home Office Furniture, Display Cases You Can Build* and *Building Woodshop Workstations*.

His Web site address is www.cabinet-making.com, and he can be reached by e-mail at danny@cabinetmaking.com.

acknowledgements | Many suppliers have contributed products, material and technical support during the project-building phase of this book — companies like Delta, Porter-Cable, Exaktor Tools, Blum and many others.

I appreciate how helpful they've been and recommend these companies without hesitation. A complete list of suppliers is included at the end of this book.

table of contents

introduction

This book is a revision of my original edition published in 1997. It contains updated information about hardware, sheet material and techniques. We've printed the book in color and improved the illustrations. The improvements in this revised text are in many ways largely due to comments I've received from readers over the last five years.

Kitchen cabinetmaking, like many other skills, requires nothing more than attention to detail and patience. This skill is learned and improved upon with practice and, I believe, well within the scope of most home woodworkers.

The kitchen cabinetmaking style detailed in this book is a simple, straightforward style used by many cabinet manufacturers, with some minor variations. Common dimensions such as cabinet depth, height and width, are detailed, as well as simple rules to calculate door widths. As you will see in later chapters, the normal depth for a base cabinet is 24", upper cabinets are approximately 12" deep, and the space between the upper and lower cabinet is from 16" to 18".

This building style was adapted from many sources. Primarily, it's a blend of the best features of European– and North American–style cabinetry. The carcass, or cabinet, is built with ⅝" or ¾" melamine-coated particleboard (PB) or veneered sheet materials. A hardwood face frame is installed, taking the place of the European method of edge tape on the exposed PB edges. Adjustable legs are installed on the base cabinets to maximize the cutting from a sheet of PB and allow for easy installation.

The hidden hinge is another European innovation used because of its strength, durability and ease of adjustment. The building system is logical and extremely adaptable to all situations, and the end result equals the best kitchen cabinets available on the market.

Building kitchen cabinets requires basic woodworking skills along with some of the power and hand tools most woodworkers own. Power tools include a table saw, circular saw, router and drills. Tools such as a radial-arm saw, power screwdrivers and power sanders are always handy but not absolutely necessary. Obviously, the more tools you have and the more experienced you are with these tools, the easier it will be to build cabinets. However, the end result is dependent on the care and attention to detail that you put into the project and not primarily on the tools you own.

The most important piece of advice that I can give anyone involves the planning and cutting of the cabinet parts. Take your time to plan the cutting process and accurately cut all the parts to the correct size. The assembly and final finishing will be simple if the cabinet pieces are accurately cut.

I have been involved in many areas of renovation work over the last 30 years, including home building, additions, basement finishing and kitchen and bathroom projects. The range has included building and installing a simple bathroom vanity to building a complete home. Over the last 5 years my specialty has been writing about kitchen cabinets and the business of cabinetmaking. I also teach a kitchen cabinetmaking course at a local college, so I'm exposed to the hands-on construction techniques.

Today the focus of activity in the home is the kitchen or family room. We seem to be reverting to earlier times when the kitchen was a large meeting place for family and friends, as well as a place to prepare meals. Consequently, over the last few years the emphasis seems to be moving toward larger kitchen and kitchen/family room combinations. New homes are being designed with larger kitchens and family or great rooms, as they are sometimes called, to meet those desires. Renovation projects involving the kitchen require more space be allocated or, at the very least, the use of light–colored or natural wood cabinets, to make the room seem larger.

Most of the kitchens in the homes of the fifties and sixties were designed with no-nonsense, dark cabinets, simply as a place to quickly prepare a meal and leave. Now everyone wants to "hang out" in the kitchen. Remember the last time you had family and friends over for a meal? Where did everyone congregate? If it's anything like my place, all the guests were in the kitchen. We don't want a dark dungeon anymore. Most of us want a bright, airy, warm and comfortable room to prepare meals, chat with friends, make crafts or just relax in a cozy surrounding.

From a personal point of view, I agree: Nothing is nicer than a large, bright, cozy kitchen. From a business point of view, I couldn't agree more; millions of older homes are waiting for a kitchen renovation. Many of us are saving for the day when we can begin a kitchen renovation project.

To illustrate my point about the popularity of kitchen renovations, take a look in the yellow pages of the phone book under "Kitchen Cabinets" and count the number of companies in your area. As well, look at most of the popular how-to shows on television and take

note of the time given to kitchen projects. It's a popular topic with most homeowners. Almost every time I meet someone new and he or she asks what I do for a living, the first comment is "That's interesting. You know, I really must do something about our kitchen."

Years ago kitchen cabinets were built without too much thought about interior use and function. Shelves were fixed in place and finished with a coat of paint. Most cabinets required the homeowner to paint the kitchen walls that could be seen inside the cabinets and cover the shelves with paper.

Today, modern kitchens have many appliances, work-saving devices and accessories that are a must in every kitchen. Pasta makers, bread makers, dishwashers, automatic coffeemakers and so on all require space in the kitchen. Modern cabinets are fitted with drawer pullouts, lazy Susans, pullouts in lower cabinets, multiple drawer assemblies, wall ovens, built-in cooktops and all the other features that make today's kitchen an exciting place to work and gather with friends.

Building kitchen cabinets is not difficult. All that is required is attention to

detail and accurate cutting. Assembly of all the parts is simple when they are sized correctly. With a little time and effort your final product will be beautiful. With this book you can build yourself a beautiful, quality kitchen and stop there, or you can build for friends and family to recoup your costs. If you really enjoy the building process, you can open your own part-time or full-time kitchen cabinetmaking business. The choice is yours. There certainly is enough work to go around for the quality kitchen cabinetmaker.

DESIGNING AND BUILDING YOUR OWN KITCHEN CABINETS

PLANNING YOUR KITCHEN

No renovation is more disruptive to a family's lifestyle than a major kitchen renovation project. Most family members spend a great portion of their time at home in the kitchen. This important room is used to prepare meals, for informal eating and as a casual gathering place for family and friends. People soon realize how important the room is when it's torn apart during renovations; even the simple task of making a cup of coffee becomes a major undertaking without a kitchen.

It's critically important that tear-out and new cabinet installation are coordinated during the design phase to minimize downtime. The last thing you want to tell someone is that the kitchen will be down another week because you forgot to order something or your dimensions were wrong and you have to rebuild a cabinet.

Most experts agree that a kitchen renovation project will return almost 100 percent on investment when the property is sold. Surveys by the real estate industry show that a kitchen is one of the most, if not the most, important feature with potential purchasers. Real estate agents have told me that the quality of the kitchen often makes or breaks the sale.

Kitchen design is subjective. Few hard and fast rules exist. A feature or layout that is perfect for one person is far from perfect for another. The issue of lifestyle and how it revolves around the kitchen is unique to each family. In most cases, the family will have definite ideas about what they want and what they would like to see in the end result. Often they have been looking through magazines, drawing rough floor plans, measuring and dreaming about their ideal kitchen for quite some time.

During the initial look at your existing kitchen, research all the information about new products and features on the market. Ask yourself questions about your requirements and put ideas on paper. Combine your notes and rough drawings along with accurate measurements and attempt to come up with two or three floor plans. I try not to radically alter anything that will change a major feature important to my family. However, I will look at alternatives if I see something that is unsafe or poorly designed. Try to incorporate the most important desires in alternative plans.

You should address a few issues during your initial look at the kitchen. Ask questions so that you understand all the needs. Consultants call it a needs-analysis study, and although I don't go in for fancy titles, I think the term applies in this case.

defining your needs

You will discover some interesting issues with this basic self-test.

1. Discuss the existing kitchen space and layout with all the primary users of the kitchen in your household, listing the good and bad points of the design.

2. Investigate the traffic patterns in and through the kitchen.

3. Analyze the day-to-day meal preparation tasks. Try to formulate a normal daily meal preparation routine.

4. Ask questions about your family's desire to do more in the kitchen. Is there a hobby or area of interest, such as baking, that you would like to do more of if the added space or facilities were available?

5. Do you feel that a lot of walking or movement is necessary during meal preparation?

6. Ask whether cleaning up after meals seems to be a monumental task. You may not solve that problem, but it may be reduced by simple layout changes.

7. Do you or your family want to entertain more casually in the kitchen and formally in the dining room if the kitchen space and functionality of the room could be improved upon?

8. Determine how long you plan to own the house. A $20,000 kitchen renovation project may not be fully recoverable if the intention is to upgrade for a quick sale in the near future. If you convince yourself to overimprove and the return is not realized during resale, you may be wasting a good deal of money.

9. Discuss your family's wish list. If space or money were no object, what would you like to have in your dream kitchen?

10. Discuss topics such as lighting, area and task illumination, kitchen seating needs, as well as appliance upgrade needs.

Kitchen design is based on personal and individual tastes. I've found being a good listener and asking many questions to be the best approach.

Two design rules that seem to be true in every case deal with color and illumination. Light-colored or natural wood cabinets tend to brighten and visually enlarge a space, and task lighting always enhances the project. Today's lifestyle is much more focused on the kitchen as a gathering place for a wide and varied number of activities.

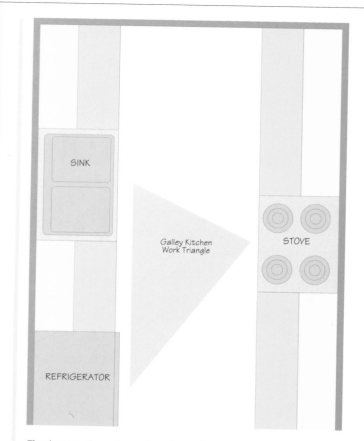

The drawing above shows the galley-style kitchen.

KITCHEN STYLES

Kitchen layouts include many styles, such as the L-shaped, galley, U-shaped and island styles. Most kitchen designers use a work triangle (see illustrations) formed by distances between the refrigerator to the stove to the sink and back to the refrigerator. The sum of the legs in the work triangle should not be less than 10' and not greater than 25'. If this sum is too small, people will be tripping over each other, and if too large, food preparation could be a tiring task.

Kitchen design has become such an important function that the National Kitchen and Bath Association (www.nkba.org) sponsors a Certified Kitchen Designer certification program. Individuals who are certified usually specialize in this area exclusively, which illustrates how vast the kitchen renovation field has become.

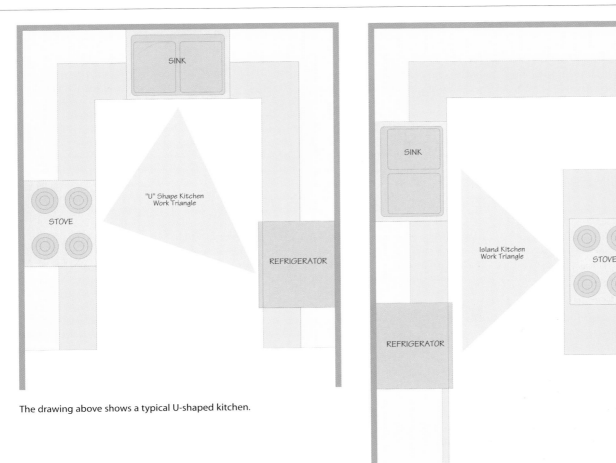

The drawing above shows a typical U-shaped kitchen.

The island kitchen is very popular when designing for a large room.

KITCHEN DESIGN STANDARDS

Most cabinetmakers follow commonly accepted standards for cabinet dimensions, including counter height, space allowance between base and upper cabinets, cabinet depth, as well as the space required for refrigerators and stoves.

These dimensions are not cast in stone but are generally accepted in the industry, particularly by accessory and appliance manufacturers when designing their products. For example, many refrigerators require 33" for proper installation, and the width of the majority of stoves is 30". Normally, a 31" space is designed into the plan for stove installation. This gives us $1/2$" on each side of the stove so that it can be easily removed and replaced during cleaning or repair.

KITCHEN CABINET CONSTRUCTION SYSTEM

The cabinet design detailed in this book is a modular blend of European and North American cabinet construction methods. The final product, once installed, looks more traditional because of the use of the face frame on the cabinet. (The main difference between North American traditional and European-style cabinetry is the use of the face frame.) European cabinetry, in general, uses the same carcass style as is used in this design, after which the exposed carcass edges are covered with veneer tape or a laminate.

The modular cabinet box (carcass) is the heart of this system.

The cabinet uppers and bases are built with ⁵/₈"- or ³/₄"-thick melamine particleboard (PB). The backs are a full ⁵/₈"- or ³/₄"-thick particleboard. Base and upper backing allows easier installation and a tighter cabinet and eliminates the need to paint the walls inside and behind the cabinets.

Modifications or special cabinet material can be substituted when the need arises. These include using wood-veneer-covered PB for microwave, pantry or glass door cabinets whose interiors will be exposed. This cabinet design is so flexible that almost all special situations can be addressed with only minor changes.

Various composite boards and hardwoods are used to build the cabinets. Shown are melamine particleboard, wood-veneer-covered particleboard, veneer plywood and hardwood for the face frames.

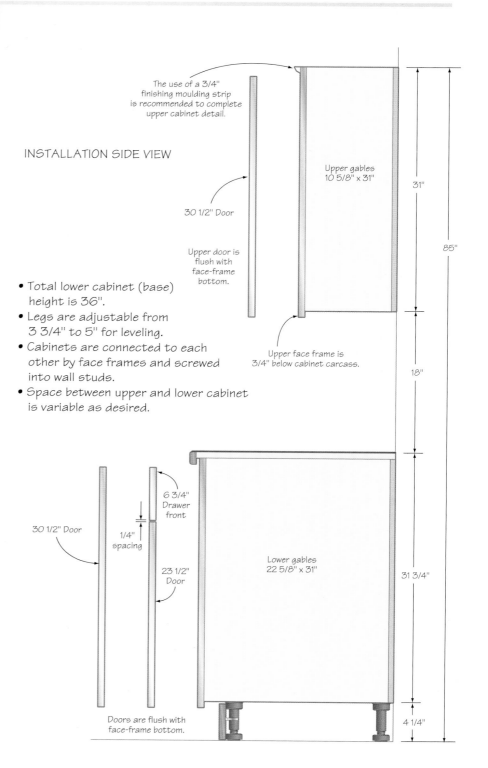

INSTALLATION SIDE VIEW

The use of a 3/4" finishing moulding strip is recommended to complete upper cabinet detail.

Upper gables 10 5/8" x 31"

30 1/2" Door

Upper door is flush with face-frame bottom.

Upper face frame is 3/4" below cabinet carcass.

31"

85"

18"

- Total lower cabinet (base) height is 36".
- Legs are adjustable from 3 3/4" to 5" for leveling.
- Cabinets are connected to each other by face frames and screwed into wall studs.
- Space between upper and lower cabinet is variable as desired.

30 1/2" Door

1/4" spacing

6 3/4" Drawer front

23 1/2" Door

Lower gables 22 5/8" x 31"

31 3/4"

4 1/4"

Doors are flush with face-frame bottom.

CABINET DOORS — BUILDING OR BUYING?

For years, prior to this kitchen cabinet design system, I made my own doors. The door styles are numerous, and I spent a great deal of time and money investing in wood shapers and bits, as well as designing and building the necessary templates. When a large kitchen renovation project requires upwards of 30 doors, construction costs are a serious consideration and can affect the profit line. In the case of solid doors, labor for gluing up blanks, shaping and cutting adds up quickly. More often than not, the next client wants a totally different door style!

For this reason, I now normally purchase factory-made doors. The companies that supply doors are numerous, their lines are varied, the cost is attractive, and you have an almost unlimited choice of door styles.

You may want to design and build your own doors, however, particularly if time is not an issue. I'll detail the process for building your own doors later in this book.

CABINET DESIGN

These cabinets have been designed without a center stile. Therefore, when the cabinet doors are open, in the case of a two-door cabinet, you have complete access to the interior. This is made possible by the use of the fully adjustable European hinge. Each of the doors can be adjusted so that there is a $1/16$" gap between them when closed. European hinges are installed on each door in a 35mm hole drilled on the inside of the door. The cabinet sides, also called the gable ends, of the standard upper and base cabinets are the same length at 31" long. Only the widths are different: $10^5/8$" wide for the uppers and $22^5/8$" wide for the base units with $5/8$"-thick PB. These dimensions allow for maximum use of a 4' × 8' standard sheet of melamine-coated particleboard for carcass construction. The melamine sheets are 97" long which gives us three sides ($3 × 31$" = 93" in total), and the side widths of the standard cabinet allow for four upper sides

The doors for this kitchen were made using $3/4$"-thick oak-veneer particleboard with taped wood-veneer edges.

Painted medium-density fiberboard (MDF) doors are a low-cost option. A new and popular option is the thermofoil (plastic-covered MDF) doors.

Five-piece wood cabinet doors with solid raised panels are the most expensive door style. Substituting the solid-wood core for a $1/4$"-thick veneer plywood center panel can reduce the price.

or two base sides across the 49" width of the sheet. The interior depth of the standard uppers are $10^5/8$" plus the face-frame thickness of $3/4$" for a total interior depth of $11^3/8$" and an interior base depth of $23^3/8$" using $5/8$"-thick PB.

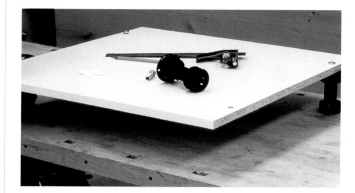

Cabinet legs allow us to use 31" cabinet sides for both the upper and lower cabinets. These legs are independently adjustable and allow for a solid piece of 1×4 hardwood board to be clipped on as the kickboard. Installation is easy and accurate.

Here is a corner base cabinet with a 32" lazy Susan installed. Base cabinets can also be constructed with one adjustable shelf, or one and two pullout drawer assemblies, depending on your needs.

Complete access to the upper cabinet space is possible because it has no center stile. The shelves are adjustable, and the melamine interiors are easy to clean.

This photo shows an upper corner cabinet equipped with an 18" round lazy Susan.

construction tip

Most professional cabinetmakers use a cabinet-grade melamine-coated particleboard. Three main grades are available: 100, 120 and 140.

I prefer the 120-grade board for the majority of my cabinetwork with this material. However, manufacturers have different grade numbering systems, so ask for details where you purchase your material.

Be aware, you can find some less-expensive melamine PB on the market. While they seem like a good buy, they are more likely to scratch and break. The particles are coarse and the glue is poor. Ask for cabinet-grade material when purchasing sheet goods.

PB is formed with glue and wood particles. The melamine surface is a paper coating that has been soaked in resin and bonded to the board to make it scratch resistant.

The high glue content makes this board very hard and, as many people who use high-speed steel tools have discovered, can ruin a saw blade or tool bit quickly. It's therefore a wise investment to use carbide-tipped cutting tools when working with this material.

Additionally, screws will hold properly only if the board has been predrilled. A hole will allow the screw to cut a thread and grip tightly. Without a pilot hole, the board may split. And there is a special screw for particleboard joinery. The shaft is thin and the threads are coarse. This allows the screw to cut a deep, well-defined threaded hole, forming an amazingly tight joint.

The completed upper cabinets are traditional in appearance and have room for plates, glasses, spices and food products.

PARTICLEBOARD MATERIAL

Make certain you buy cabinet-grade melamine particleboard. Investigate the supply in your area and buy the highest grade available; it is cheaper in the long run. If the supplier doesn't know the grade they stock, check the distributors lists on two of the largest manufacturer's Web sites: Uniboard Canada, Inc. at www.uniboard.com and Panolam Industries at www.panolam.com.

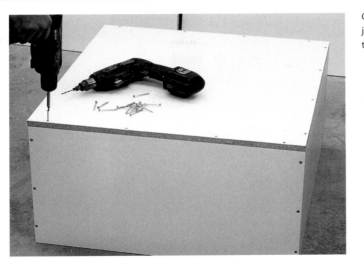

Carcasses are butt joined with 2" particleboard screws.

Four joinery systems are used to join particleboard and plywood veneer panels. From left to right: the particleboard screw, confirmat screw, biscuit and dowel.

The most common joinery system is the particleboard or chipboard screws available at most large home centers and through the sources at the end of this book. The wood face frame is constructed using butt joints, glue and two wood screws at each joint. Other joinery options include biscuits, pocket screws on the rear of the face frame or a mortise-and-tenon joint. This wood face frame is then attached to the carcass front using glue and 2" finishing nails. Nails are countersunk and the holes are covered with colored wood filler wax, making them almost invisible. If you want to avoid nailing and filling, you can use biscuits. However, under normal circumstances, the cabinet door covers the filled nail holes.

The cabinets in this system use an adjustable shelf as the standard. It provides you with an efficient and flexible cabinet. Normally, I install two adjustable shelves in each standard upper cabinet with an $1\frac{1}{4}$" (32mm) position adjustment.

Plastic cap moulding is available at most home stores and is an ideal protective front edge covering for shelves.

construction tip

If the shelving is greater than 30" wide, I often install a 1×2 hardwood cleat, running the full width of the shelf, on the rear underside of the shelf board, for added rigidity. You can also use $\frac{3}{4}$"-thick material for these longer shelves. The front or exposed edge of the PB can be covered with a plastic edging called cap moulding or with white iron-on edge tape. You can also face the shelf with hardwood. I normally construct full-depth base shelves to maximize the storage space of the cabinet.

DRAWERS

Drawers are constructed with many types of materials. Melamine particleboard is one option that can be used to build a solid, maintenance-free drawer.

Drawers are an important and integral component in any kitchen renovation project. The majority of kitchens have a four-drawer bank for cutlery and utensils, plus additional drawers in the base cabinets. Microwave cabinets with a lower drawer bank are also an extremely popular addition to the modern kitchen.

In keeping with the design of the cabinets, I wanted to construct drawers that were sturdy, reasonably priced and easy to maintain (the melamine surface is easy to clean), since the drawer would be opened and closed many thousands of times throughout the life of the kitchen. The cost of manufacturing a lot of drawers for the typical kitchen is an important issue. Solid-wood drawers would be strong but expensive, so a construction method based on melamine-coated particleboard seemed to be the answer.

After cutting out the cabinet body parts, use the remaining PB and 2" PB screws to construct the drawer boxes. The exposed top edge of the melamine PB for the drawer box can be covered with matching iron-on veneer tape or with $1/4$"-thick solid-wood strips, which are rounded over and finished. The wood edge on the drawers is the same wood as the cabinets and is an attractive accent detail when the drawer is opened. European drawer glides are used to mount the drawers in the cabinets. A wood front is attached to the box, acting as the drawer face, and is either purchased from your cabinet door supplier or made to match the doors you are installing.

I have been using this method of construction for about 8 years, and I have not had any drawer problems. The drawer carcass is heavy due to the weight of the PB material, making it operate smoothly.

Baltic birch plywood, which is sometimes called cabinet-grade plywood, and solid hardwoods to match the wood you've chosen to build your kitchen can also be used to construct drawer boxes.

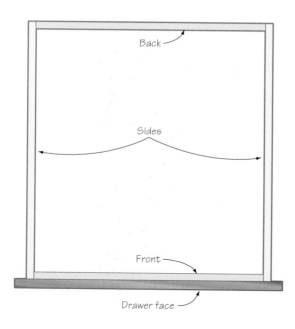

DRAWER CARCASS ASSEMBLY

Back

Sides

Front

Drawer face

TOP VIEW

Drawer face — Wood edge

Drawer back

Drawer side

RIGHT-SIDE VIEW

Drawer Carcass and Front Assembly

• PB drawer sides are screwed to back and front boards.

• Leave side screws flush with surface to cover with plastic caps.

• Cover edge of drawer bottom board along each side with melamine tape.

• Drawer carcass is 1" less in width and 1" less in height than drawer opening.

pullouts | Base cabinet pullouts greatly increase the storage capacity of a cabinet and allow easy access to all the items on the shelf.

Base cabinet pullouts can be a $5/8$" or $3/4$" melamine PB box, much like the drawer carcass, with a solid-wood face. A few options I've used include solid-wood pullouts with rails, melamine PB with hardwood rails and extra-deep pullouts for garbage and recycling bins.

drawers | Drawers are an important part of any kitchen project. Melamine drawer boxes are attractive and easy to keep clean.

bathroom cabinets | Bathroom cabinets can be built using these kitchen cabinet construction methods. The counter heights are typically lower on bathroom cabinets, so adjust the side and backboard dimensions to suit your requirements.

Bathroom renovations are as popular as kitchen renovations. Wood cabinets, in light, natural finishes, seem to be the style of choice. Bathrooms, like kitchens, are being given more space during the design process in new construction and renovation projects in existing homes. The trend seems to be toward larger, brighter and more functional bathrooms with whirlpools, shower stalls, drawer banks, corner cabinets and pantry units.

All the standard cutting and assembly principles can be applied when building custom bathroom cabinets. The only major difference is the cabinet height, which ranges from 28" to 36". A cabinet height of 34" appears to be the most popular. Cabinets over the sink base can be 6" to 10" deep.

The adjustable-leg feature of this cabinet system is a benefit in a bathroom application because heating, plumbing and electrical installation needs, often a problem in the confined bathroom space, are more effectively met because of the added space under the cabinets.

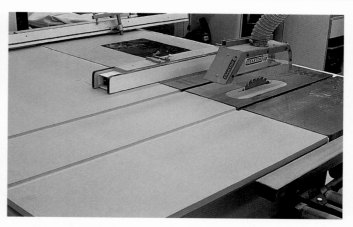

table saw | The table saw is my most important asset in the shop. Cutting 4' x 8' sheets of particleboard or plywood with anything other than a table saw is a difficult job. Nothing can match the accuracy and consistency of this tool.

support rollers & tables | Infeed and outfeed rollers on your table saw improve cuts and reduce fatigue. Tables can be made simply or you can purchase roller assemblies.

blades | Generally, it's important that your cutting equipment is carbide tipped. Saw blades, countersink and router bits will last much longer than high-speed steel when cutting the high-glue-content particleboards. Though initially more expensive, carbide-tipped tools will cost less in the long run.

Some degree of edge chip on melamine-coated particleboard is a fact of life when cutting this material. However, near perfect cuts can be achieved by using a dedicated melamine PB cutting blade.

table saw slide table | A table saw accessory called a slide table is a nice option when crosscutting ripped panels to size. Another method that I often use is to cut the sheet into slightly oversize pieces with a circular saw, then trim these easier-to-handle smaller sections of the sheet to the exact size.

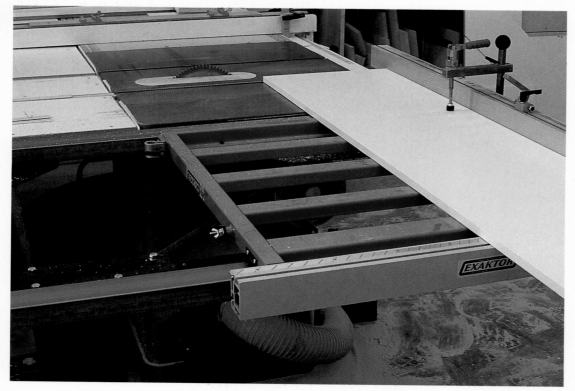

routers | A heavy-duty plunge router is ideal and versatile. It's well worth considering if you plan to purchase one router.

Small laminate trim routers are easy to handle and work extremely well when you have to flush-trim high-pressure laminate material. However, any size router will accomplish this task.

cordless drill/ driver | The cordless screwdriver makes screw insertion go much faster. They are invaluable in a kitchen project that normally requires between 500 and 1,000 screws!

drill press | The 35mm flat-bottom hole in the door, used for hinge mounting, is best made with a drill press. The unit doesn't have to be large or fancy; it simply has to hold the drill bit at a right angle to the door.

power sanders | Power sanders in the random-orbit and palm style are a good investment. I rough-sand with 100- and 150-grit papers on the random-orbit sander and finish with 180-grit paper by hand and with the palm sander.

KITCHEN CABINET ANATOMY

CABINET PART NAMES

An upper cabinet carcass is made up of five pieces: two sides, a back, top and bottom. The standard base is constructed with two sides, a back and a bottom. The base units have adjustable legs and don't require a top, because the countertop sits on the cabinet.

hybrid cabinet parts | A hardwood face frame is constructed and installed to replace the European method of taping the PB edges on a frameless-style carcass. This face frame gives the cabinet a North American appearance. Face-frame components consist of vertical members called stiles and horizontal members called rails.

21

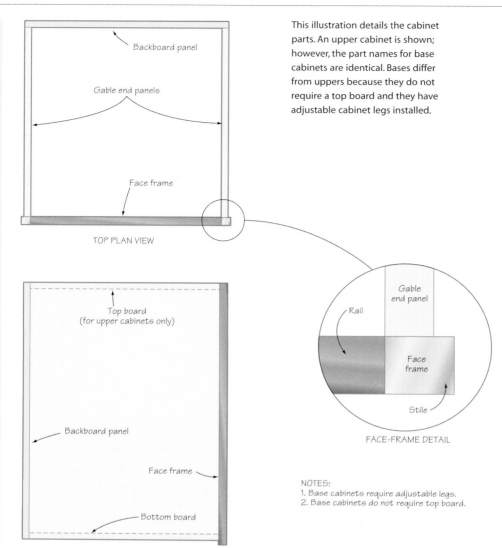

Backboard panel

Gable end panels

Face frame

TOP PLAN VIEW

Top board
(for upper cabinets only)

Backboard panel

Face frame

Bottom board

LEFT-SIDE VIEW

This illustration details the cabinet parts. An upper cabinet is shown; however, the part names for base cabinets are identical. Bases differ from uppers because they do not require a top board and they have adjustable cabinet legs installed.

Gable
end panel

Rail

Face
frame

Stile

FACE-FRAME DETAIL

NOTES:
1. Base cabinets require adjustable legs.
2. Base cabinets do not require top board.

european hinge | European door hinges can be adjusted in three directions. The design of this hinge allows for accurate placement of the cabinet doors. Hinges are classified by degrees of opening. A 90° hinge will allow the door to swing fully open at a right angle to the face frame. There are also 100°- to 180°-opening hinges. Corner base cabinets with a lazy Susan installed require a wider degree of door opening to provide easy access to the cabinet.

drawer glides | European drawer glides consist of two drawer runners and two cabinet-side runners. You do not have to build hardwood drawer rails to support the hardware.

adjustable legs | Cabinet legs come in many styles. One common model is attached to the cabinet base with four $^5/_8$" screws through holes in the leg flange. The kick plate simply clips onto the leg with an assembly called a plinth clip.

BENEFITS OF USING ADJUSTABLE LEG ASSEMBLIES

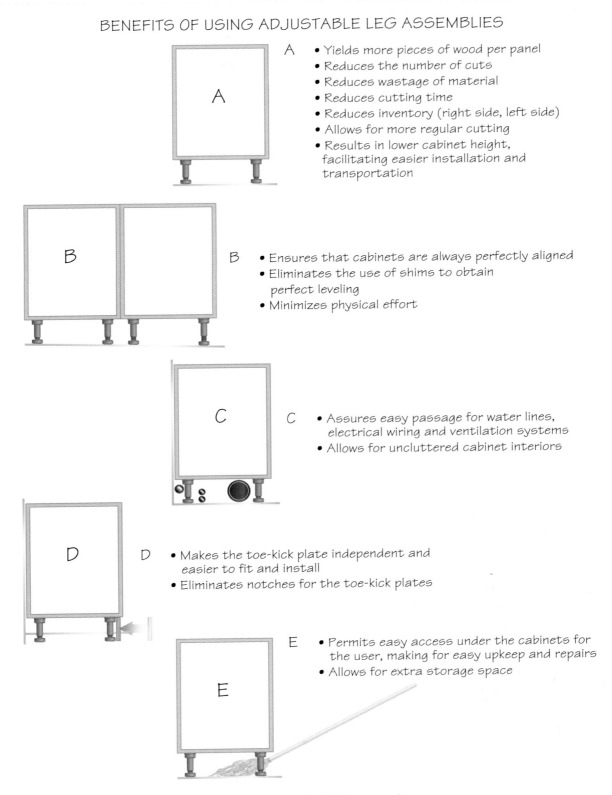

A
- Yields more pieces of wood per panel
- Reduces the number of cuts
- Reduces wastage of material
- Reduces cutting time
- Reduces inventory (right side, left side)
- Allows for more regular cutting
- Results in lower cabinet height, facilitating easier installation and transportation

B
- Ensures that cabinets are always perfectly aligned
- Eliminates the use of shims to obtain perfect leveling
- Minimizes physical effort

C
- Assures easy passage for water lines, electrical wiring and ventilation systems
- Allows for uncluttered cabinet interiors

D
- Makes the toe-kick plate independent and easier to fit and install
- Eliminates notches for the toe-kick plates

E
- Permits easy access under the cabinets for the user, making for easy upkeep and repairs
- Allows for extra storage space

Adjustable cabinet legs on the base cabinets, which are used extensively in this building system, change the traditional side design. In systems without the legs, the sides are longer and require a notch to provide the undercabinet clearance called the kick space.

When the side isn't seen, the traditional method is to build a base support frame of 2×4 lumber. That traditional method is strong, but gives rise to installation problems when the floor isn't level. You're required to shim the base frame support until you have a level surface, which is very time-consuming.

CONSTRUCTION PRINCIPLES

The standard upper cabinet is the most basic cabinet in this building system.

The sides or gable ends of the cabinet perform some important functions. Primarily, of course, they define the height of the cabinet box and give it strength. The sides also support the European hidden hinges and are drilled for the shelf support pins. Also, in this particular cabinet style, the face frame is nailed onto the side edges as well as the top and bottom board edges.

The bottom and top boards of the cabinet carcass form the box shape of the cabinet in conjunction with the sides. More importantly, the bottom and top boards define the interior width of the carcass. Be careful to cut these two boards to the proper dimensions. Interior width is important because the doors, and the resulting door overlay, are calculated based on the inside dimension of the cabinet. This measurement determines combined door width, hinge style and individual door width.

Cabinet sides are cut to a length of 31", and the face-frame stiles are cut at $31\frac{3}{4}$". This is done so the face frame hangs $\frac{3}{4}$" below the carcass bottom. This feature gives a little flexibility when assembling cabinets and hides the edge of finish boards that will be applied under the cabinet.

Standard doors are $30\frac{1}{2}$" high and mounted flush with the bottom of the face frame, leaving a $1\frac{1}{4}$" gap at the top of the cabinet for installation of edge moulding.

You'll want to remember a number of principles when creating a materials cutting list for your upper cabinets. The top and bottom boards are always 2" narrower than the cabinet exterior on this face-frame design. Cabinet width is measured at the widest point on the front of the cabinet. The stiles are each 1" wide, so if the cabinet we

BUILDING UPPER FACE-FRAME CABINETS

want to build is 30" wide, our bottom and top boards are 28" wide. This will make the inside face of each stile flush with the inside face of the cabinet sides, permitting us to use European hinges.

The stiles are $^3/_4$" longer than the cabinet sides, and the face-frame rails are the same width as the cabinet bottom and top boards. The backboard is equal to the cabinet's inside dimension plus the two thicknesses of side boards. For example, on a 30" cabinet using $^5/_8$"-thick sheet material, our backboard must be $29^1/_4$" wide.

The standard upper cabinets usually have two shelves installed on adjustable

pins. The shelves are cut $^1/_{16}$" shorter than the bottom boards to make them easier to install and move. Door width, or one door on narrow cabinets, is determined by adding 1" to the interior width. If you need only one door, that's the final width. If two doors are needed, divide the interior-width-plus-1" formula by two. A 30" cabinet would need two $14^1/_2$"-wide doors.

I want to be sure that the inside edges of my stiles fully cover the cabinet's side edges. It wouldn't look good if a bit of the carcass side's front edge was showing. To guarantee total coverage every time, the bottom and

top boards, or the bottom board in the case of base cabinets, are cut $^1/_{16}$" wider than required. As well, I always cut the backboards $^1/_8$" more than needed as they can be accurately trimmed before installing them on the carcasses. The veneer bottom panel on upper cabinets is cut slightly narrower than the bottom so it can be installed after the cabinet is assembled.

A slight overhang of $^1/_{32}$" on each stile inside the cabinet will not affect hinge installation. And I can always measure the assembled sides and bottom board's width and cut the backboard to the proper dimension.

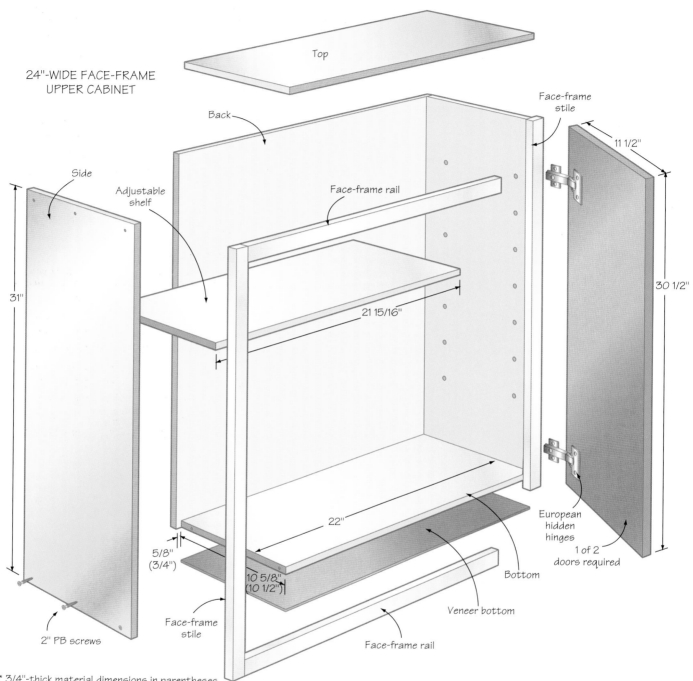

24"-WIDE FACE-FRAME
UPPER CABINET

Top

Back

Side

Adjustable
shelf

Face-frame rail

Face-frame
stile

11 1/2"

30 1/2"

31"

21 15/16"

European
hidden
hinges

1 of 2
doors required

22"

5/8"
(3/4")

10 5/8"
(10 1/2")

Bottom

Veneer bottom

Face-frame
stile

Face-frame rail

2" PB screws

* 3/4"-thick material dimensions in parentheses

CUTTING LIST FOR UPPER CABINETS USING $^5/_8$" (16MM) THICK SHEET MATERIAL – INCHES (MILLIMETERS)

CABINET WIDTH	CABINET BOX			FACE FRAME		DOOR WIDTH 30$^1/_2$" HIGH (775)
	TWO SIDES DEPTH × HEIGHT	TOP & BOTTOM DEPTH × WIDTH	ONE BACK WIDTH × HEIGHT	TWO STILES WIDTH × HEIGHT	TWO RAILS HEIGHT × WIDTH	
12 (305)	10$^5/_8$ × 31 (270 × 787)	10$^5/_8$ × 10$^1/_{16}$ (270 × 256)	11$^7/_{16}$ × 31 (290 × 787)	1 × 31$^3/_4$ (25 × 806)	1$^1/_2$ × 10 (38 × 254)	1 @ 11 (279)
15 (381)	10$^5/_8$ × 31 (270 × 787)	10$^5/_8$ × 13$^1/_{16}$ (270 × 332)	14$^7/_{16}$ × 31 (367 × 787)	1 × 31$^3/_4$ (25 × 806)	1$^1/_2$ × 13 (38 × 330)	1 @ 14 (356)
18 (457)	10$^5/_8$ × 31 (270 × 787)	10$^5/_8$ × 16$^1/_{16}$ (270 × 408)	17$^7/_{16}$ × 31 (443 × 787)	1 × 31$^3/_4$ (25 × 806)	1$^1/_2$ × 16 (38 × 406)	1 @ 17 (432)
21 (533)	10$^5/_8$ × 31 (270 × 787)	10$^5/_8$ × 19$^1/_{16}$ (270 × 485)	20$^7/_{16}$ × 31 (519 × 787)	1 × 31$^3/_4$ (25 × 806)	1$^1/_2$ × 19 (38 × 483)	2 @ 10 (254)
24 (610)	10$^5/_8$ × 31 (270 × 787)	10$^5/_8$ × 22$^1/_{16}$ (270 × 561)	23$^7/_{16}$ × 31 (595 × 787)	1 × 31$^3/_4$ (25 × 806)	1$^1/_2$ × 22 (38 × 559)	2 @ 11$^1/_2$ (292)
27 (686)	10$^5/_8$ × 31 (270 × 787)	10$^5/_8$ × 25$^1/_{16}$ (270 × 637)	26$^7/_{16}$ × 31 (671 × 787)	1 × 31$^3/_4$ (25 × 806)	1$^1/_2$ × 25 (38 × 635)	2 @ 13 (330)
30 (762)	10$^5/_8$ × 31 (270 × 787)	10$^5/_8$ × 28$^1/_{16}$ (270 × 713)	29$^7/_{16}$ × 31 (748 × 787)	1 × 31$^3/_4$ (25 × 806)	1$^1/_2$ × 28 (38 × 711)	2 @ 14$^1/_2$ (369)
33 (838)	10$^5/_8$ × 31 (270 × 787)	10$^5/_8$ × 31$^1/_{16}$ (270 × 789)	32$^7/_{16}$ × 31 (824 × 787)	1 × 31$^3/_4$ (25 × 806)	1$^1/_2$ × 31 (38 × 787)	2 @ 16 (406)
36 (914)	10$^5/_8$ × 31 (270 × 787)	10$^5/_8$ × 34$^1/_{16}$ (270 × 866)	35$^7/_{16}$ × 31 (900 × 787)	1 × 31$^3/_4$ (25 × 806)	1$^1/_2$ × 34 (38 × 864)	2 @ 17$^1/_2$ (445)

CUTTING LIST FOR UPPER CABINETS USING $^3/_4$" (19MM) THICK SHEET MATERIAL – INCHES (MILLIMETERS)

CABINET WIDTH	CABINET BOX			FACE FRAME		DOOR WIDTH 30$^1/_2$" HIGH (775)
	TWO SIDES DEPTH × HEIGHT	TOP & BOTTOM DEPTH × WIDTH	ONE BACK WIDTH × HEIGHT	TWO STILES WIDTH × HEIGHT	TWO RAILS HEIGHT × WIDTH	
12 (305)	10$^1/_2$ × 31 (267 × 787)	10$^1/_2$ × 10$^1/_{16}$ (267 × 256)	11$^{11}/_{16}$ × 31 (297 × 787)	1 × 31$^3/_4$ (25 × 806)	1$^1/_2$ × 10 (38 × 254)	1 @ 11 (279)
15 (381)	10$^1/_2$ × 31 (267 × 787)	10$^1/_2$ × 13$^1/_{16}$ (267 × 332)	14$^{11}/_{16}$ × 31 (374 × 787)	1 × 31$^3/_4$ (25 × 806)	1$^1/_2$ × 13 (38 × 330)	1 @ 14 (356)
18 (457)	10$^1/_2$ x 31 (267 × 787)	10$^1/_2$ × 16$^1/_{16}$ (267 × 408)	17$^{11}/_{16}$ × 31 (450 × 787)	1 × 31$^3/_4$ (25 × 806)	1$^1/_2$ × 16 (38 × 406)	1 @ 17 (432)
21 (533)	10$^1/_2$ × 31 (267 × 787)	10$^1/_2$ × 19$^1/_{16}$ (267 × 485)	20$^{11}/_{16}$ × 31 (526 × 787)	1 × 31$^3/_4$ (25 × 806)	1$^1/_2$ × 19 (38 × 483)	2 @ 10 (254)
24 (610)	10$^1/_2$ × 31 (267 × 787)	10$^1/_2$ × 22$^1/_{16}$ (267 × 561)	23$^{11}/_{16}$ × 31 (602 × 787)	1 × 31$^3/_4$ (25 × 806)	1$^1/_2$ × 22 (38 × 559)	2 @ 11$^1/_2$ (292)
27 (686)	10$^1/_2$ × 31 (267 × 787)	10$^1/_2$ × 25$^1/_{16}$ (267 × 637)	26$^{11}/_{16}$ × 31 (678 × 787)	1 × 31$^3/_4$ (25 × 806)	1$^1/_2$ × 25 (38 × 635)	2 @ 13 (330)
30 (762)	10$^1/_2$ × 31 (267 × 787)	10$^1/_2$ × 28$^1/_{16}$ (267 × 713)	29$^{11}/_{16}$ × 31 (755 × 787)	1 × 31$^3/_4$ (25 × 806)	1$^1/_2$ × 28 (38 × 711)	2 @ 14$^1/_2$ (369)
33 (838)	10$^1/_2$ × 31 (267 × 787)	10$^1/_2$ × 31$^1/_{16}$ (267 × 789)	32$^{11}/_{16}$ × 31 (831 × 787)	1 × 31$^3/_4$ (25 × 806)	1$^1/_2$ × 31 (38 × 787)	2 @ 16 (406)
36 (814)	10$^1/_2$ × 31 (267 × 787)	10$^1/_2$ × 34$^1/_{16}$ (267 × 866)	35$^{11}/_{16}$ × 31 (907 × 787)	1 × 31$^3/_4$ (25 × 806)	1$^1/_2$ × 34 (38 × 864)	2 @ 17$^1/_2$ (445)

CABINET SIZES

Two cutting lists are shown. One is for construction of standard upper cabinets using $^5/_8$"-thick material, and the other is for $^3/_4$"-thick material. They are sample widths; however, the components for any cabinet width can be calculated by following the construction principles.

Building the Standard Upper Face-Frame Cabinet

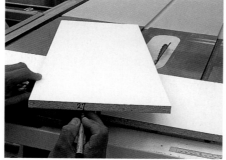

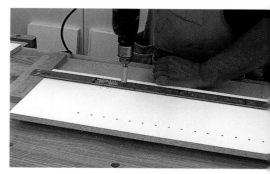

1 Rip and crosscut the stiles and rails. Assemble each frame using glue and 2"-long screws in counterbored pilot holes. If the screw hole will be visible, fill the $^3/_8$" counterbore with a wood plug. You can also use pocket holes, mortise-and-tenon joints, dowels or miniature biscuits to assemble the face frame.

The face frames are constructed and sanded now so they can have two or three coats of finish applied. You can do the finishing while assembling cabinet carcasses so the face frame will be ready when it's time to attach it. Don't put any finish on the back face of the face frame so the glue can bond properly.

2 Cut the carcass parts to size. Number the parts as detailed on your cutting list and illustrations following the procedures described in chapter twelve.

3 Drill the holes in each side board for the adjustable shelves, if needed. Be sure to mark the top of each panel. I normally start and end my columns of holes 4" from the top and bottom edges. The hole columns are placed 1" in from the back and front edges and are the diameter required for the shelf pins you plan to use. See the sidebar "Building a Shelf-Pin-Hole Drilling Jig."

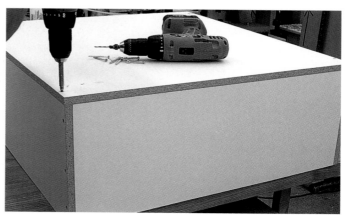

4 Fasten one side board to the edge of the bottom board. Drill a $^1/_8$" countersunk pilot hole for each of the three 2" PB screws. Connect the remaining three corner butt joints in the same manner. Normally, with this face-frame style of cabinetry, the end gables that are exposed on any side will have a $^1/_4$"-thick veneer plywood covering to match the wood on the cabinet doors and face frames.

5 For purposes of verification at this point, referencing a 30" upper cabinet as an example, you should have a four-sided box with inside dimensions of $28^1/_{16}$" wide (the width of the bottom and top carcass boards) by $29^3/_4$" high (the length of the side minus the thickness of the top and bottom carcass boards when using $^5/_8$" sheet material).

Now, measure the actual width of the carcass. If the sheet material is slightly thicker than $^5/_8$" or $^3/_4$", or your cutting on the top and bottom boards was a little strong, your carcass will be wider than planned. However, the backboard was cut slightly wider to accommodate that possibility. Trim the back to the correct size before attaching it to the carcass.

Secure the backboard to the carcass, flush with all edges of the box. This will force the cabinet corners into square. Install 2" PB screws at 6" centers around the perimeter of the back. Secure the first corner, aligning it square, then secure the remaining three corners while aligning the box. Install screws between the corners, aligning the sides, bottom and top boards flush with the edge of the backboard. Always drill pilot holes for the screws. Use a marking gauge to draw lines $^5/_{16}$" in from the edges as a guide for the pilot holes.

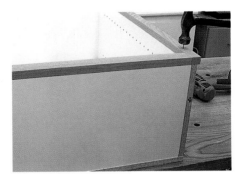

6 | Apply glue to the four carcass edges and place the face frame's outside top edge flush with the outside top edges of the carcass. The face frame should fully cover the carcass edges; it should, in fact, be slightly smaller on the inside dimension versus the inside dimension of the carcass. As detailed earlier, the carcass bottom and top are cut $^1/_{16}$" larger than the face-frame rails to guarantee full carcass edge coverage by the face frame. Divide the difference between the two inside edges. Secure the top corner of the face frame to the carcass body using 2" finishing nails in pilot holes slightly smaller than the nail diameter. Drill the pilot hole so that it centers on the PB edge.

Secure the other top corner so that the top outside edge of the face frame is flush with the top outside edge of the carcass. Then, nail the bottom two corners, making sure that the slight overhang of the face frame inside the carcass is maintained equally on both sides. Install the remaining nails at 8" centers. The bottom rail should hang below the cabinet carcass by $^3/_4$". When building with $^5/_8$"-thick sheet material, the sides of the face frame should extend $^3/_8$" beyond each side of the carcass; the sides should extend $^1/_4$" for $^3/_4$"-thick sheet goods. Also, the inside edge of the bottom rail will be slightly above the bottom board with $^5/_8$" sheets, and flush with the top face of the bottom board when using $^3/_4$"-thick sheet material.

If you don't like nailing the face frames, use biscuits for an invisible joint. Remember though, the door, in its normally open or closed position, covers the section of the face frame where the nails are located.

7 | Pick the style of door you would like to install. Buy the doors from a supplier, or refer to chapter nine and build your own doors. Door heights for standard cabinets with this building system are $30^1/_2$" high. The width of each door is dependent on the size of the carcass. Use the 1" rule to determine the door width required: The doors are 1" wider than the inside stile-to-stile distance. If you require two doors, simply divide the door width required by two. For example, a 24"-wide face-frame upper has an inside dimension of 22". Add 1" and divide by two (22" + 1" = 23" divided by 2 = $11^1/_2$"), meaning each door will be $11^1/_2$" wide.

8 | Drill a 35mm-diameter hole, 3" on center, from each end of the door. The edge of the hole should be $^1/_8$" away from the door's edge. Use a hinge-boring bit to drill the hole $^1/_2$" deep, or as specified by the hinge supplier.

Attach a 100° to 120° standard-opening hinge with two $^5/_8$" screws, using a square to make sure the hinge arm is at 90° to the door's edge. Once the hinges are secure, attach the mounting plate to each hinge.

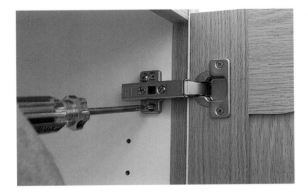

9 | Hold the door in its normally open position, with the hinge and plate attached to the door, and place a $^1/_8$"-thick spacer between the face-frame stile and back edge of the door. Drive screws through the hinge plate and into the cabinet side to secure the doors.

The doors adjust sideways, up and down, as well as closer or farther away from the cabinet. On many hinges, the screw closest to the door moves the door side to side, the farthest screw is used to minimize the gap between the cabinet edge and door. The hinge plate has a screw that can be loosened to move the door up and down. (See the adjustment instructions for your particular hinge.) Adjust both doors so the reveal is equal on both sides and there is a $^1/_{16}$" gap between doors on a two-door cabinet.

To complete the standard upper cabinet, install shelf pins, test fit the shelves and attach handles or knobs of your choice. The shelf's front edge can be covered with iron-on melamine edge tape, cap moulding that's available at the home store or wood edge trim to match the doors.

building a shelf-pin-hole drilling jig

This jig is a handy shop tool. It will act as a guide for drilling accurately placed holes in cabinet sides up to 31" long. The flat steel is available at most hardware stores. All the other materials required are readily available from any home store.

1 Cut a piece of $^3/_4$" plywood that's 13" wide and $34^1/_{16}$" long. Attach two boards that are $^3/_4$" thick by $1^1/_2$" wide by 10" long. Use four $1^1/_4$"-long screws per board. Install the boards flush at each end so there is $31^1/_{16}$" between them.

2 To help keep the cabinet sides oriented properly, mark the jig as shown. I note the top of the cabinet side with an X when drilling shelf holes on each board's edge.

3 Prepare a piece of $^1/_4$"-thick flat steel that's $1^1/_2$" wide by 34" long. Drill holes at $1^1/_4$" on center up the middle of the bar. If you prefer, you can increase or decrease the hole spacing. You should also decide which shelf pin you will be using and drill the guide holes to the diameter required for those pins. Locate two holes at either end of the flat steel and attach it to the end boards with $1^1/_2$" screws.

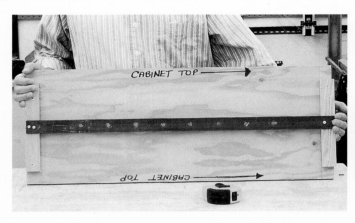

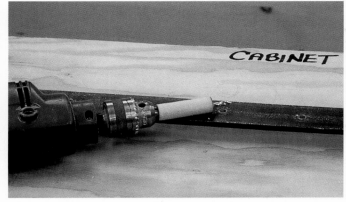

4 The jig will accept cabinet sides up to $^3/_4$" thick and 31" long. If you want to drill shorter sides, put spacers in the jig to hold the cabinet side tight against the top board.

Drill one vertical set of holes and move the cabinet side over to drill the other set. Normally, each cabinet side will require two parallel sets of holes. Guide marks on the jig's end boards will help position the holes 1" in from each side board's edge.

5 Drilling through a piece of dowel rod makes a simple drill depth stop. Set the drill bit in the chuck, with the stop in place, so the bit can travel through the steel and approximately three-quarters of the way through a cabinet side. The stop will prevent the drill bit from exiting the finished face of the cabinet side. Make sure the hole is deep enough for the shelf pin to be properly seated and secure.

SHELF-PIN-HOLE DRILLING JIG

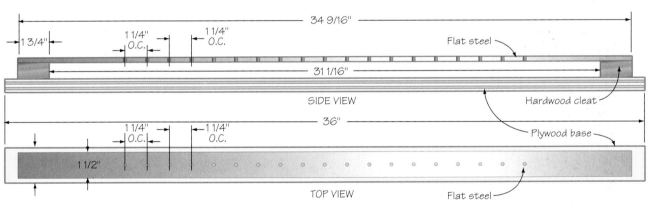

Leave 31 1/16" for gable end placement.
Drill 3/16" holes in the flat steel at 1 1/4" on center to guide drill bit.
Drill shelf-pin holes in gable ends at 1" from each edge.

Building a 24" Upper Corner Cabinet

An upper corner cabinet with a lazy Susan assembly is a popular and useful addition in any kitchen renovation project.

This cabinet is called a 24" upper corner because it covers 24" on each wall of a corner. The face is 45° to the cabinets on either side. Dead space, often found in corner wall cabinets, is minimized by the installation of a lazy Susan assembly.

Face-frame members need to be cut at $22\frac{1}{2}°$ angles so the two parts of each stile form a 45° angle. Cut the top and bottom boards to the size stated in the table, leaving the angle cut until you are ready to assemble the pieces.

As illustrated in the cutting list, pay particular attention to the backboard cut sizes. One back is $\frac{5}{8}"$ or $\frac{3}{4}"$ wider to allow for the required overlaps of the boards during assembly.

1 Six panels are required for this cabinet. It is almost always fitted with a two-shelf, 18"-diameter round lazy Susan assembly, and therefore holes for adjustable shelves are not required. Mark the angle cuts on the top and bottom boards.

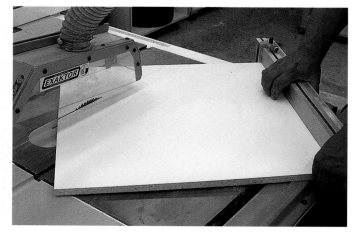

2 If you have a sliding table on your saw, or an angle-cutting jig, prepare the boards as indicated in the drawing. You can cut the front angles with a circular saw or jigsaw, keeping $\frac{1}{8}"$ away from the line, then dress the boards to the line with a belt sander. Take your time and you'll get an accurate cut with minimum chipping of the melamine coating.

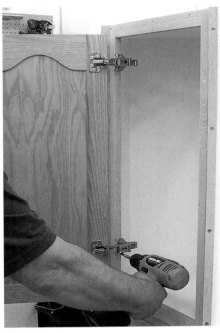

3 Assemble the boards as shown in the drawing, making sure all joints are square. Note the position of the backboards and how each one overlaps at the corners during assembly.

4 Cut the six wood parts for the face frame and assemble as indicated. Use angle clamps to help hold the stiles in place while they are glued and screwed to each other. I normally attach the two inside stiles to the rails with glue and screws first. Then I secure the two outside stiles to the inside stiles, making sure the angle cuts are properly aligned with each other, using glue and four 1$^1/_2$" screws per side.

You won't need a $^1/_8$" spacer when installing the upper corner cabinet door using 170° hinges and face-frame mounting plates. Two small hooks on the face-frame mounting plate align it correctly on the inside edge of the stile.

construction tip

5 Glue and nail the face frame to the carcass as shown. Install the frame with the outside top edge flush with the outside top of the carcass. The inside surface of the stiles is not flush with the sides as in the other cabinets, so a special face-frame hinge plate is used to secure the hinges and door for this cabinet.

6 Two 170°-opening hinges are used for this cabinet door. The wide-opening hinges allow the door to swing farther so the cabinet can be easily accessed. The hinges attach to the inside edge of one stile with special face-frame hinge plates.

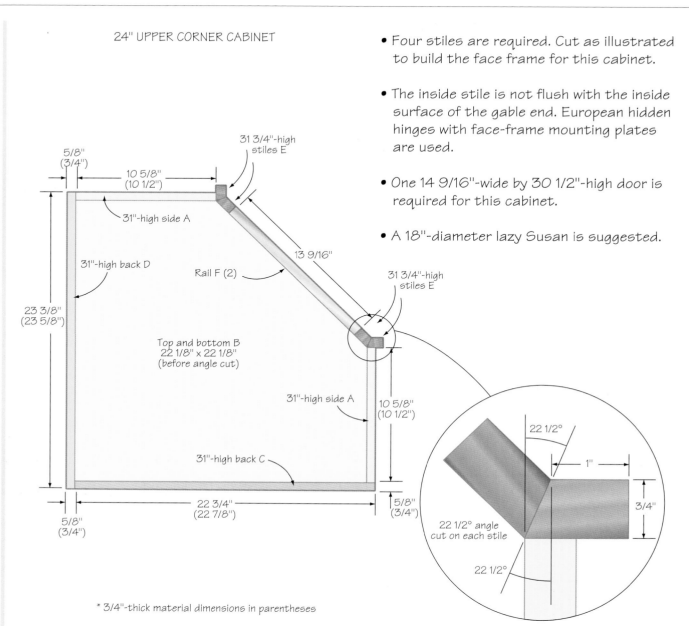

24" UPPER CORNER CABINET

5/8"
(3/4")

10 5/8"
(10 1/2")

31 3/4"-high
stiles E

31"-high side A

31"-high back D

Rail F (2)

13 9/16"

31 3/4"-high
stiles E

23 3/8"
(23 5/8")

Top and bottom B
22 1/8" x 22 1/8"
(before angle cut)

31"-high side A

10 5/8"
(10 1/2")

31"-high back C

5/8"
(3/4")

22 3/4"
(22 7/8")

5/8"
(3/4")

22 1/2°

1"

3/4"

22 1/2° angle
cut on each stile

22 1/2°

* 3/4"-thick material dimensions in parentheses

- Four stiles are required. Cut as illustrated to build the face frame for this cabinet.

- The inside stile is not flush with the inside surface of the gable end. European hidden hinges with face-frame mounting plates are used.

- One 14 9/16"-wide by 30 1/2"-high door is required for this cabinet.

- A 18"-diameter lazy Susan is suggested.

shop tip

Use a combination square set at half the thickness of the boards you are using to mark a screw-hole line as a guide for accurate drilling. How do you know what one-half of ⁵⁄₈" or ³⁄₄" or even ¹¹⁄₁₆" is? For that matter, any fraction? Simply double the bottom number of the fraction and that's half the distance. Try it out — half of ⁵⁄₈" is ⁵⁄₁₆", ³⁄₄" is ³⁄₈", ¹¹⁄₁₆" is ¹¹⁄₃₂", and so on. It works every time!

CUTTING LIST FOR A 24" (610MM) UPPER CORNER CABINET USING $^5/_8$" (16MM) THICK SHEET MATERIAL

inches (millimeters)

REFERENCE	QUANTITY	PART	STOCK	THICKNESS	(mm)	WIDTH	(mm)	LENGTH	(mm)	COMMENTS
A	2	sides	melamine pb	$^5/_8$	(16)	$10^5/_8$	(270)	31	(787)	
B	2	top & bottom	melamine pb	$^5/_8$	(16)	$22^1/_8$	(562)	$22^1/_8$	(562)	cut as illustrated
C	1	back	melamine pb	$^5/_8$	(16)	$22^3/_4$	(578)	31	(787)	
D	1	back	melamine pb	$^5/_8$	(16)	$23^3/_8$	(594)	31	(787)	
E	4	stiles	hardwood	$^3/_4$	(19)	$1^1/_2$	(38)	$31^3/_4$	(806)	rip at $22^1/_2°$ on one edge with a 1"(25mm)-wide front face
F	2	rails	hardwood	$^3/_4$	(19)	$1^1/_2$	(38)	$13^9/_{16}$	(344)	
G	1	door		$^3/_4$	(19)	$14^9/_{16}$	(370)	$30^1/_2$-high	(775)	stock can be veneer pb or frame and panel hardwood

CUTTING LIST FOR A 24" (610MM) UPPER CORNER CABINET USING $^3/_4$" (19MM) THICK SHEET MATERIAL

inches (millimeters)

REFERENCE	QUANTITY	PART	STOCK	THICKNESS	(mm)	WIDTH	(mm)	LENGTH	(mm)	COMMENTS
A	2	sides	melamine pb	$^3/_4$	(19)	$10^1/_2$	(267)	31	(787)	
B	2	top & bottom	melamine pb	$^3/_4$	(19)	$22^1/_8$	(562)	$22^1/_8$	(562)	cut as illustrated
C	1	back	melamine pb	$^3/_4$	(19)	$22^7/_8$	(581)	31	(787)	
D	1	back	melamine pb	$^3/_4$	(19)	$23^5/_8$	(600)	31	(787)	
E	4	stiles	hardwood	$^3/_4$	(19)	$1^1/_2$	(38)	$31^3/_4$	(806)	rip at $22^1/_2°$ on one edge with a 1"(25mm)-wide front face
F	2	rails	hardwood	$^3/_4$	(19)	$1^1/_2$	(38)	$13^9/_{16}$	(344)	
G	1	door		$^3/_4$	(19)	$14^9/_{16}$	(370)	$30^1/_2$-high	(775)	stock can be veneer pb or frame and panel hardwood

OVER-THE-STOVE UPPER CABINETS

Stove cabinets are not as large as standard upper cabinets because a range hood is normally mounted under the cabinet and greater clearance between the stove and the upper cabinet is required to properly work at the stove.

I normally install a 30"-wide by 19¼"-high cabinet with 18"-high doors. These measurements are for cabinets over standard-size stoves. I use a 30"-wide cabinet with ½" added to the adjoining stiles of the cabinets on either side. I want the space between the base units that are on each side of the stove to be 31", and the wider upper stiles will let me accomplish this when the base cabinets are aligned with the uppers. I can then overhang my countertop ³⁄₈" on each base cabinet to the right and left of the stove, which allows for a maximum opening, between the countertop ends, of 30¼" for the stove. Widening the cabinet stiles on the right and left of the stove upper permits countertop overhang and allows for proper clearance of the stove, as well as aligning the doors on the upper and lower cabinets on each side of the stove.

To custom design any size over-the-stove cabinet, you need the following design dimensions for upper cabinets. The basic rules of the inside width of the face frame equaling the inside width of the cabinet carcass (top and bottom board), the face frame being ¾" greater than the cabinet carcass in total height, and the doors being 1¼" less than the face-frame height, determine your cabinet dimensions. The door width equals the inside cabinet dimension plus 1" and, in the case of this 30" reduced-height upper, divide by two to find the width of each door.

The stove cabinet I normally use follows these rules. The face frame is

19¼" high, with two 14½"-wide by 18"-high doors, the inside carcass width is 28", and the sides are 18½" high. The backboard is the width of the bottom board plus the two thicknesses of the side boards. If you were using ⁵⁄₈"-thick sheet material, the backboard would be 29¼" wide by 18½" high. The ¾" material would mean a backboard that's 29½" wide by 18½" high. The 28" inside cabinet width plus the total width of the two 1" stiles equals a cabinet that is 30" wide.

OVER-THE-FRIDGE UPPER CABINETS

I use two sizes of cabinets as over-the-fridge cabinets. You have a choice based on your requirements.

The majority of refrigerators on the market today are 31" to 32" wide, so my normal cabinet width for either style is 33". I use a standard maximum cabinet height of 85" made up of a 36" base unit and countertop height, plus 18" countertop surface to the bottom of the upper cabinet distance, and 31" upper cabinet height. I want the top of the fridge cabinet even with the uppers at that 85" height. Refrigerators are approximately 65" high, leaving a clearance of about 20" for a cabinet above the appliance.

Your choice depends on how much clearance you would like between the bottom of the cabinet and the top of the fridge. A 17$\frac{1}{4}$" cabinet with 16"-high standard doors will leave a 2$\frac{3}{4}$" space, and a 14$\frac{1}{4}$" cabinet with 13"-high standard doors will leave a 5$\frac{3}{4}$" space.

Calculating parts for any cabinet can be easily accomplished by working backwards from the door dimension. The over-the-fridge cabinet, called a 17$\frac{1}{4}$"-high upper (the height of the face-frame stiles), takes 16"-high doors. We know, based on the standard design rules, that there is a 1$\frac{1}{4}$" space above the door, therefore our face frame is 17$\frac{1}{4}$" high.

Each door is 16". Since the stiles on a regular face frame are 1" wide, the bottom and top board of this cabinet must be 31" wide. Also, the standard face frame hangs $\frac{3}{4}$" below the cabinet bottom and is flush with the top, so our sides must be 16$\frac{1}{2}$" high. The backboard is the height of the sides and as wide as the bottom or top board plus the thickness of the two sides. Backboard width for $\frac{5}{8}$"-thick sheet stock is 32$\frac{1}{4}$", and 31$\frac{1}{2}$" when $\frac{3}{4}$"-thick sheet material is used.

Cabinet depth on this upper is a matter of personal choice. Some people like the look of a recessed cabinet (standard 12" depth) over the fridge, while others want a cabinet flush with the appliance door. Simply adjust the depth of the sides, top and bottom board while taking into account the thickness of the face frame and the cabinet door to get the desired total cabinet depth.

OVER-THE-SINK UPPER CABINETS

Clearance is required when working at the sink, therefore over-the-sink cabinets, when installed, are not normally full-height cabinets. Standard widths are used (a 36"-wide cabinet in most cases); however, the height is the same as the over-the-stove cabinet at 19$\frac{1}{4}$".

This reduced-height sink upper is by no means a hard-and-fast design rule. I have used both standard full-height and reduced-height uppers over the sink. I will usually install undercabinet lighting on this cabinet, as discussed in chapter six. In kitchens without a window over the sink cabinet, task lighting is a practical feature.

CONSTRUCTION PRINCIPLES

The standard base face-frame cabinet differs from the standard upper face-frame cabinet in two areas — the lack of a carcass top board and the addition of adjustable legs.

No top board is needed, as the kitchen countertop covers the base cabinet. The countertop is secured with screws and right-angle clips. This method, along with the face frame, gives the installed base cabinet its strength and rigidity. I use $\frac{3}{4}" \times \frac{3}{4}"$ metal right-angle clips, two per side, two on the backboard, and one in the center of the face-frame rail. The countertop is secured with two $\frac{5}{8}"$ screws through each right-angle clip.

Adjustable cabinet legs are used, replacing the base frame that was common with older-style kitchens. These legs simplify cabinet installation and hold the kick plate by means of special clips called plinth clips. The adjustable cabinet legs are popular and can be purchased at kitchen hardware supply stores. The total cost of the legs for each cabinet is greater than the cost of the material for a wood base. However, the building time for the base, when added to the difficulty of cabinet installation, justifies the few extra dollars.

Most legs adjust from $3\frac{3}{4}"$ to $5"$ in height. In effect, the kitchen floor would have to be out of level by more than 1" before the legs require shims.

Base cabinets are multifunction units. They are equipped with adjustable shelves, pullout shelf assemblies, drawers or other special features such as trash and recycling containers. Holes for the adjustable shelves are drilled in the carcass sides by the same method, and with the same jig assembly, as the standard upper cabinets. Drawers and pullouts are easily installed using the European bottom-mount drawer-glide hardware.

Accessories for kitchen base cabinets, such as pullout wire baskets, towel racks, laundry hampers, double,

BUILDING BASE FACE-FRAME CABINETS

triple and quadruple recycling bin systems, as well as flip-out ironing boards and work-center platforms, can be found in most home centers.

Remember the principles of construction that I detailed for the upper cabinets. The bottom board is always 2" narrower than the cabinet exterior on this face-frame design. Cabinet width is always measured at the widest point on the front of the cabinet. For example, if the cabinet we want to build is 30" wide and we know that the stiles are each 1" wide, our bottom board is 28" wide. This will make the inside face of each stile flush with the inside face of the cabinet sides, allowing

us to use European hinges.

The stiles are $^{3}/_{4}$" longer than the cabinet sides, and the face-frame rails are $^{1}/_{16}$" narrower than the cabinet bottom board. The backboard is equal to the cabinet's inside dimension plus the two thicknesses of side boards. For a 30" cabinet, our backboard must be $29^{1}/_{4}$" wide when building with $^{5}/_{8}$" sheet material.

The backboard is cut $^{1}/_{8}$" wider than the total width of the bottom board plus the two side thicknesses. This is a first cut when I'm ripping all my sheet materials to size. If there is any thickness variance in the sheet material, most often thicker than the stated $^{5}/_{8}$" or $^{3}/_{4}$",

I will be able to trim the width after measuring the assembled box and before I attach the backboard.

Standard base cabinets usually have one shelf installed on adjustable pins. The shelves are cut $^{1}/_{16}$" narrower than the bottom boards to make them easier to install and move. Door width is determined by adding 1" to the interior width. If it's only one door, that's the final width. If two doors are needed, divide the interior-width-plus-1" formula by two. A 30" cabinet would need two $14^{1}/_{2}$"-wide doors mounted on European hidden hinges.

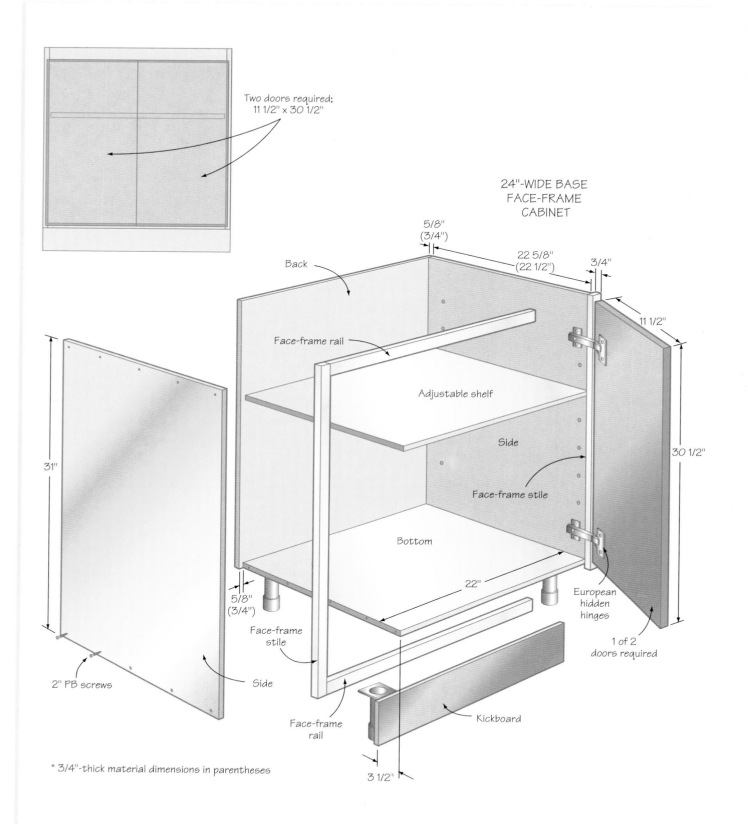

Two doors required:
11 1/2" x 30 1/2"

24"-WIDE BASE
FACE-FRAME
CABINET

5/8"
(3/4")

22 5/8"
(22 1/2")

3/4"

Back

11 1/2"

Face-frame rail

Adjustable shelf

Side

30 1/2"

Face-frame stile

31"

Bottom

22"

European
hidden
hinges

5/8"
(3/4")

1 of 2
doors required

Face-frame
stile

2" PB screws

Side

Face-frame
rail

Kickboard

3 1/2"

* 3/4"-thick material dimensions in parentheses

CUTTING LIST FOR UPPER CABINETS USING $5/8$"-THICK (16MM) SHEET MATERIAL – INCHES (MILLIMETERS)

CABINET WIDTH	CABINET BOX			FACE FRAME		DOOR WIDTH 30$1/2$" HIGH (775)
	TWO SIDES DEPTH x HEIGHT	TOP & BOTTOM DEPTH x WIDTH	ONE BACK WIDTH x HEIGHT	TWO STILES WIDTH x HEIGHT	TWO RAILS HEIGHT x WIDTH	
12 (305)	$22^5/8 \times 31$ (575 × 787)	$22^5/8 \times 10^1/16$ (575 × 256)	$11^7/16 \times 31$ (290 × 787)	$1 \times 31^3/4$ (25 × 806)	$1^1/2 \times 10$ (38 × 254)	1 @ 11 (279)
15 (381)	$22^5/8 \times 31$ (575 × 787)	$22^5/8 \times 13^1/16$ (575 × 332)	$14^7/16 \times 31$ (367 × 787)	$1 \times 31^3/4$ (25 × 806)	$1^1/2 \times 13$ (38 × 330)	1 @ 14 (356)
18 (457)	$22^5/8 \times 31$ (575 × 787)	$22^5/8 \times 16^1/16$ (575 × 408)	$17^7/16 \times 31$ (443 × 787)	$1 \times 31^3/4$ (25 × 806)	$1^1/2 \times 16$ (38 × 406)	1 @ 17 (432)
21 (533)	$22^5/8 \times 31$ (575 × 787)	$22^5/8 \times 19^1/16$ (575 × 485)	$20^7/16 \times 31$ (519 × 787)	$1 \times 31^3/4$ (25 × 806)	$1^1/2 \times 19$ (38 × 483)	2 @ 10 (254)
24 (610)	$22^5/8 \times 31$ (575 × 787)	$22^5/8 \times 22^1/16$ (575 × 561)	$23^7/16 \times 31$ (595 × 787)	$1 \times 31^3/4$ (25 × 806)	$1^1/2 \times 22$ (38 × 559)	2 @ 11$1/2$ (292)
27 (686)	$22^5/8 \times 31$ (575 × 787)	$22^5/8 \times 25^1/16$ (575 × 637)	$26^7/16 \times 31$ (671 × 787)	$1 \times 31^3/4$ (25 × 806)	$1^1/2 \times 25$ (38 × 635)	2 @ 13 (330)
30 (762)	$22^5/8 \times 31$ (575 × 787)	$22^5/8 \times 28^1/16$ (575 × 713)	$29^7/16 \times 31$ (748 × 787)	$1 \times 31^3/4$ (25 × 806)	$1^1/2 \times 28$ (38 × 711)	2 @ 14$1/2$ (369)
33 (838)	$22^5/8 \times 31$ (575 × 787)	$22^5/8 \times 31^1/16$ (575 × 789)	$32^7/16 \times 31$ (824 × 787)	$1 \times 31^3/4$ (25 × 806)	$1^1/2 \times 31$ (38 × 787)	2 @ 16 (406)
36 (914)	$22^5/8 \times 31$ (575 × 787)	$22^5/8 \times 34^1/16$ (575 × 866)	$35^7/16 \times 31$ (900 × 787)	$1 \times 31^3/4$ (25 × 806)	$1^1/2 \times 34$ (38 × 864)	2 @ 17$1/2$ (445)

CUTTING LIST FOR BASE CABINETS USING $3/4$"-THICK (19MM) SHEET MATERIAL – INCHES (MILLIMETERS)

CABINET WIDTH	CABINET BOX			FACE FRAME		DOOR WIDTH 30$1/2$" HIGH (775)
	TWO SIDES DEPTH x HEIGHT	TOP & BOTTOM DEPTH x WIDTH	ONE BACK WIDTH x HEIGHT	TWO STILES WIDTH x HEIGHT	TWO RAILS HEIGHT x WIDTH	
12 (305)	$22^1/2 \times 31$ (572 × 787)	$22^1/2 \times 10^1/16$ (572 × 256)	$11^{11}/16 \times 31$ (297 × 787)	$1 \times 31^3/4$ (25 × 806)	$1^1/2 \times 10$ (38 × 254)	1 @ 11 (279)
15 (381)	$22^1/2 \times 31$ (572 × 787)	$22^1/2 \times 13^1/16$ (572 × 332)	$14^{11}/16 \times 31$ (374 × 787)	$1 \times 31^3/4$ (25 × 806)	$1^1/2 \times 13$ (38 × 330)	1 @ 14 (356)
18 (457)	$22^1/2 \times 31$ (572 × 787)	$22^1/2 \times 16^1/16$ (572 × 408)	$17^{11}/16 \times 31$ (450 × 787)	$1 \times 31^3/4$ (25 × 806)	$1^1/2 \times 16$ (38 × 406)	1 @ 17 (432)
21 (533)	$22^1/2 \times 31$ (572 × 787)	$22^1/2 \times 19^1/16$ (572 × 485)	$20^{11}/16 \times 31$ (526 × 787)	$1 \times 31^3/4$ (25 × 806)	$1^1/2 \times 19$ (38 × 483)	2 @ 10 (254)
24 (610)	$22^1/2 \times 31$ (572 × 787)	$22^1/2 \times 22^1/16$ (572 × 561)	$23^{11}/16 \times 31$ (602 × 787)	$1 \times 31^3/4$ (25 × 806)	$1^1/2 \times 22$ (38 × 559)	2 @ 11$1/2$ (292)
27 (686)	$22^1/2 \times 31$ (572 × 787)	$22^1/2 \times 25^1/16$ (572 × 637)	$26^{11}/16 \times 31$ (678 × 787)	$1 \times 31^3/4$ (25 × 806)	$1^1/2 \times 25$ (38 × 635)	2 @ 13 (330)
30 (762)	$22^1/2 \times 31$ (572 × 787)	$22^1/2 \times 28^1/16$ (572 × 713)	$29^{11}/16 \times 31$ (755 × 787)	$1 \times 31^3/4$ (25 × 806)	$1^1/2 \times 28$ (38 × 711)	2 @ 14$1/2$ (369)
33 (838)	$22^1/2 \times 31$ (572 × 787)	$22^1/2 \times 31^1/16$ (572 × 789)	$32^{11}/16 \times 31$ (831 × 787)	$1 \times 31^3/4$ (25 × 806)	$1^1/2 \times 31$ (38 × 787)	2 @ 16 (406)
36 (914)	$22^1/2 \times 31$ (572 × 787)	$22^1/2 \times 34^1/16$ (572 × 866)	$35^{11}/16 \times 31$ (907 × 787)	$1 \times 31^3/4$ (25 × 806)	$1^1/2 \times 34$ (38 × 864)	2 @ 17$1/2$ (445)

CABINET SIZES

Two cutting lists are shown. One is for construction of standard base cabinets using $5/8$"-thick material, and the other is for $3/4$"-thick material. They are sample widths, however; the components for any cabinet width can be calculated by following the construction principles.

Building the Standard Base Face-Frame Cabinet

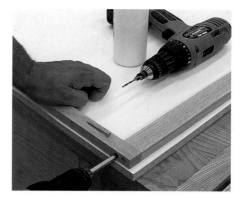

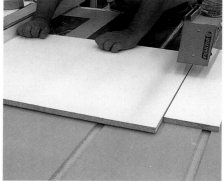

1 Rip and crosscut the stiles and rails. Assemble each frame using glue and 2"-long screws in counterbored pilot holes. If the screw hole will be visible, fill the $^3/_8$" counterbore with a wood plug. You can also use pocket holes, mortise-and-tenon joints, dowels or miniature biscuits to assemble the face frame.

The face frames are constructed and sanded now so they can have two or three coats of finish applied. You can do the finishing while assembling cabinet carcasses so the face frame will be available when it's time to attach it. Don't put any finish on the back face of the face frame so the glue can properly bond.

2 Cut the carcass parts to size. Number the parts as detailed on your cutting list and diagrams following the procedures described in chapter twelve.

3 Drill the holes in each side board for the adjustable shelf, if needed. (If you plan to install a pullout as detailed in chapter nine, shelf holes are not required.) Be sure to mark the top of each panel. I normally start and end my columns of holes 4" from the top and bottom edges. The hole columns are placed 1" in from the back and front edges and are the diameter required for the shelf pins you plan to use. You can use your shelf-pin-hole drilling jig from the previous chapter.

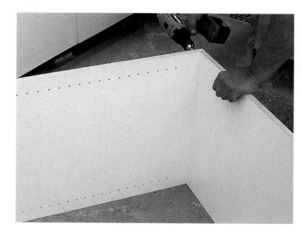

5 For purposes of verification at this point, referencing a 30" base cabinet as an example, you should have a three-sided box with inside dimensions of $28^1/_{16}$" wide (the width of the bottom board) by $30^3/_8$" high (the length of the side minus the thickness of the bottom carcass board when using $^5/_8$" sheet material).

Now, measure the actual width of the carcass. If the sheet material is slightly thicker than $^5/_8$" or $^3/_4$", or your cutting on the top and bottom boards was a little strong, your carcass will be wider than planned. However, the backboard was cut slightly wider to accommodate that possibility. Trim the back to the correct size before attaching it to the carcass.

Secure the backboard to the carcass, flush with all edges of the box. This will force the cabinet corners into square. Remember, the backboard was intentionally cut wider to accommodate thickness variances in the PB material.

Install 2" PB screws at 6" centers around the perimeter of the back. Secure upper corners first, aligning the backboard top edge to the side board's top edges, then secure the two bottom corners while aligning the box. Finally, install screws between the corners, aligning the sides and bottom boards flush with the edge of the backboard. Use a marking gauge to draw lines $^5/_{16}$" in from the edges as a guide for the pilot holes.

4 Fasten one side board to the edge of the bottom board, making sure the joint is square and flush. Drill a $^1/_8$" countersunk pilot hole for each of the four 2" PB screws. Do not overtighten or apply so much force to the screws that they strip their threaded hole. Take care as well to drill the pilot hole so that it's in the center of the edge on the board you are fastening the side to; in this case, the bottom board of the carcass. Fasten the other side board to the bottom following the same process.

Once again, you have joinery options at this point. You can use biscuits, dowels or confirmat screws. Normally, with this face-frame style of cabinetry, the end gables that are exposed on any side will have a $^1/_4$"-thick veneer plywood covering to match the wood on the cabinet doors and face frames.

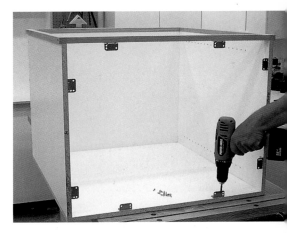

6 Apply glue to the three carcass edges and place the face frame's outside top edge flush with the outside top edges of the side boards. Align the tops of the side boards with the face frame to match the slight overhangs at the bottom of your carcass. The face frame should fully cover the carcass edges; it should, in fact, be slightly smaller on the inside dimension versus the inside dimension of the carcass. As detailed earlier, the carcass bottom is cut $^1/_{16}$" larger than the face-frame rails to guarantee full carcass edge coverage by the face frame. Divide the difference between the two inside edges. Secure the top corner of the face frame to the carcass body using 2" finishing nails in pilot holes slightly smaller than the nail thickness. Drill the pilot hole so that it centers, as much as possible, on the PB edge.

Secure the other top corner so that the top outside of the face frame is flush with the top outside edge of the carcass. Nail the bottom two corners, making sure that the slight overhang of the face frame inside the carcass is maintained equally on both sides. Install the remaining nails at 8" centers, maintaining the overhang. The bottom rail should hang below the cabinet carcass by $^3/_4$". When building with $^5/_8$"-thick sheet material, the sides of the face frame should extend $^3/_8$" beyond each side of the carcass; the sides should extend $^1/_4$" for $^3/_4$"-thick sheet goods. Also, the inside edge of the bottom rail will be slightly above the bottom board with $^5/_8$" sheets, and flush with the top face of the bottom board when using $^3/_4$"-thick sheet material.

7 Attach right-angle brackets on the carcass side and backboards, as well as the back of the upper face-frame rail. Use two brackets per section and secure them with $^5/_8$"-long screws. The bracket should be flush or slightly below the top edge of each panel, so the countertop will be drawn down to the carcass.

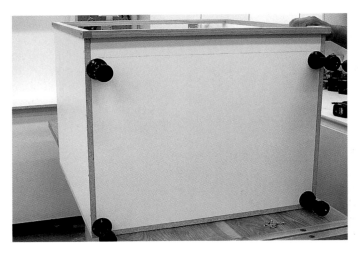

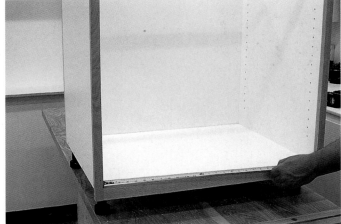

8 The cabinet legs are attached with four $^5/_8$"-long screws through the flange. The cabinet legs you purchase may not have a flange with screw holes and may require installation with a thick bolt through the cabinet bottom board. Refer to the installation instructions that came with the legs.

The leg flanges are positioned to support the back and side boards. The front legs are set back $3^1/_2$" for a kick space. If this cabinet is an end-of-run unit, open on one side, set back the legs by $3^1/_2$" on that open side as well. The kick plate is clipped to the legs with plinth clips that are screwed to the back of the board.

9 Pick the style of door you would like to install. Buy your doors from a supplier, or refer to chapter nine to build your own doors. Door heights for standard cabinets with this building system are $30^1/_2$" high. The width of each door is dependent on the size of the carcass. Use the 1" rule as discussed in previous chapters. To review, the doors are 1" wider than the inside stile-to-stile distance. If you require two doors, simply divide the door width by two. For example, a 24"-wide face-frame base has an inside dimension of 22". Add 1" and divide by two (22" + 1" = 23" divided by 2 = $11^1/_2$"), meaning each door will be $11^1/_2$" wide.

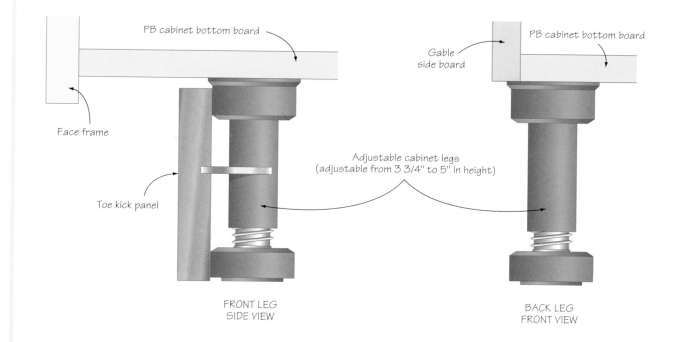

PB cabinet bottom board

Gable
side board

PB cabinet bottom board

Face frame

Toe kick panel

Adjustable cabinet legs
(adjustable from 3 3/4" to 5" in height)

FRONT LEG
SIDE VIEW

BACK LEG
FRONT VIEW

10 Drill a 35mm-diameter hole, 3" on center, from each end of the door. The edge of the hole should be $^1/_8$" away from the door's edge. Use a hinge-boring bit to drill the hole $^1/_2$" deep, or as specified by the hinge supplier.

Attach a 100° to 120° standard-opening hinge with two $^5/_8$" screws, using a square to make sure the hinge arm is at 90° to the door's edge. Once the hinges are secure, attach the mounting plate to each hinge.

11 Hold the door in its normally open position, with the hinge and plate attached to the door, and place a $^1/_8$"-thick spacer between the face-frame stile and back edge of the door. Drive screws through the hinge plate and into the cabinet side to secure the doors.

The doors adjust sideways, up and down, as well as closer or farther away from the cabinet. On many hinges, the screw closest to the door moves the door side to side, and the farthest screw is used to minimize the gap between the cabinet edge and door. The hinge plate has a screw that can be loosened to move the door up and down. (See the adjustment instructions for your particular hinge.) Adjust both doors so the reveal is equal on both sides and there is a $^1/_{16}$" gap between doors on a two-door cabinet.

To complete the standard base cabinet, install shelf pins, test fit the shelves and attach handles or knobs of your choice. The shelf's front edge can be covered with iron-on melamine edge tape, cap moulding that's available at the home store or wood edge trim to match the doors.

BUILDING A 36" CORNER BASE CABINET

One of the most popular and effective storage options for kitchens is the 36" corner base cabinet equipped with a 32" lazy Susan assembly. This cabinet eliminates the lower dead zone in base cabinets at the point where two cabinets meet in the corner. I'm sure everyone can remember crawling into a corner base to find a misplaced pot. It's frustrating, and that four square feet of space is often ignored. Unless you have a kitchen the size of a tennis court, that space is valuable real estate.

A two-shelf rotating lazy Susan assembly can be purchased at most major hardware stores. Installation is a simple matter with the supplied instructions. Major manufacturers such as Rev-A-Shelf produce a high-quality assembly that will last many years.

CUTTING LIST FOR A 36" (914MM) CORNER BASE CABINET USING ⅝" (16MM) THICK SHEET MATERIAL

inches (millimeters)

REFERENCE	QUANTITY	PART	STOCK	THICKNESS	(mm)	WIDTH	(mm)	LENGTH	(mm)	COMMENTS
A	2	sides	melamine pb	⅝	(16)	22⅝	(575)	31	(787)	
B	1	bottom	melamine pb	⅝	(16)	33⅞	(860)	33⅞	(860)	cut as illustrated
C	2	backs	melamine pb	⅝	(16)	22⅝	(575)	31	(787)	
D	1	back	melamine pb	⅝	(16)	18	(457)	31	(787)	cut oversize, then sides are angle-cut at 45° to fit
E	2	stiles	hardwood	¾	(19)	1½	(38)	31¾	(806)	
F	2	rails	hardwood	¾	(19)	1½	(38)	11¼	(285)	
G	2	rails	hardwood	¾	(19)	1½	(38)	10½	(267)	
H	2	doors		¾	(19)	10	(254)	30½-high	(775)	stock can be wood-veneer pb or frame and panel hardwood

CUTTING LIST FOR A 36" (914MM) CORNER BASE CABINET USING ¾" (19MM) THICK SHEET MATERIAL

inches (millimeters)

REFERENCE	QUANTITY	PART	STOCK	THICKNESS	(mm)	WIDTH	(mm)	LENGTH	(mm)	COMMENTS
A	2	sides	melamine pb	¾	(19)	22½	(572)	31	(787)	
B	1	bottom	melamine pb	¾	(19)	33¾	(857)	33¾	(857)	cut as illustrated
C	2	backs	melamine pb	¾	(19)	22¾	(578)	31	(787)	
D	1	back	melamine pb	¾	(19)	18	(457)	31	(787)	cut oversize, then sides are angle-cut at 45° to fit
E	2	stiles	hardwood	¾	(19)	1½	(38)	31¾	(806)	
F	2	rails	hardwood	¾	(19)	1½	(38)	11¼	(285)	
G	2	rails	hardwood	¾	(19)	1½	(38)	10½	(267)	
H	2	doors		¾	(19)	10	(254)	30½-high	(775)	stock can be wood-veneer pb or frame and panel hardwood

cutting list

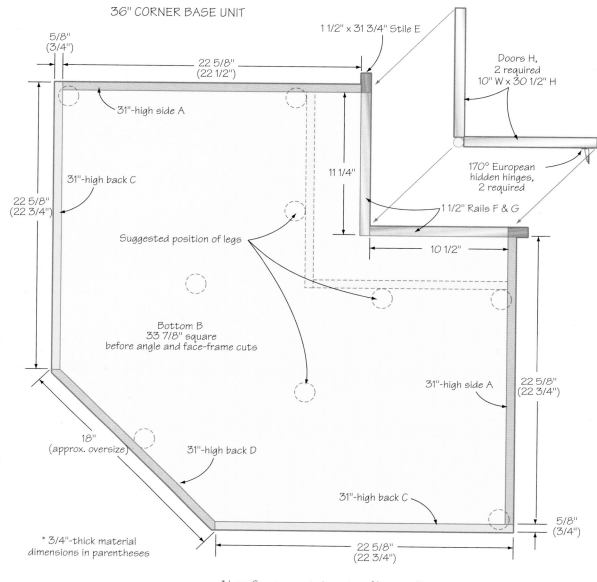

36" CORNER BASE UNIT

1 1/2" x 31 3/4" Stile E

5/8"
(3/4")

22 5/8"
(22 1/2")

Doors H,
2 required
10" W x 30 1/2" H

31"-high side A

31"-high back C

11 1/4"

170° European
hidden hinges,
2 required

1 1/2" Rails F & G

22 5/8"
(22 3/4")

Suggested position of legs

10 1/2"

Bottom B
33 7/8" square
before angle and face-frame cuts

31"-high side A

22 5/8"
(22 3/4")

18"
(approx. oversize)

31"-high back D

31"-high back C

5/8"
(3/4")

* 3/4"-thick material
dimensions in parentheses

22 5/8"
(22 3/4")

* Lazy Susan mounts in center of base and is supported on top
by a cross brace attached by PB screws to the side ends.

1 | The cabinet has six PB pieces as indicated in the drawing and in the cutting lists. Accurately cut the pieces as detailed. Do not cut the angles on the 18" × 31" backboard D at this time. I recommend that you cut it with straight cuts to the stated 18" × 31" size.

2 | Draw the front notch cutout lines and back angle cut line on the bottom B. Use a table saw to cut the two front notch lines, pushing the board in until the blade is about 3" away from the corner of the notch. The bottom of your blade will undercut farther into the board and will weaken the cutout. Follow the same procedures for the other line, running your blade into the board until it's 3" from the corner mark. Use a handsaw or jigsaw to complete the notch cutout. Next, guide the two front corners of the cutout section against the table saw fence with the fence set to a width of cut that will travel the blade along the angled back cut line. Be sure that your fence is long enough so that both cutout corners are tight against the fence for the full angled cut.

3 | Install the cabinet legs in the positions as indicated in the drawing. Maintain the 3$\frac{1}{2}$" setback from the front edges of the cabinet. Remember that this setback is required for kickboard spacing on all the base cabinets. Position the other legs so they will extend out from the edge of the bottom board by $\frac{5}{8}$" to aid in supporting the cabinet sides.

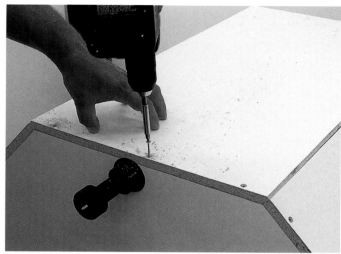

4 Assemble the cabinet boards as shown, leaving the 18" × 31" backboard D until all others are secured. Use 2" PB screws in pilot holes, spaced every 8" on each panel. As well as securing the backs and sides to the bottom board, you'll also have to secure the backs to the sides with screws at each corner.

5 Measure the opening for the backboard D and fit it to the cabinet by cutting 45° angles on each side. It may be helpful the first time you build one of these cabinets to angle-cut the backboard so that it's a little larger, and trial fit the panel. Continue cutting the backboard slightly smaller after each trial fit until it's perfect.

Use 2" PB screws to attach the angled back to the bottom boards and backboards. Carefully site the screw line through the angled back and into the edge of the backs when drilling a pilot hole. It's a little difficult to drive screws at an angle, but take your time and drill the pilot hole accurately. Three screws on each side of the panel and two into the bottom board will hold it securely.

6 Cut and assemble the face frame as indicated, and install with the inside face of the sides flush to the inside surface of the face-frame stiles. Secure the frame to the carcass with glue and 2" finishing nails.

7 Install the angle clips, two per panel, so the countertop can be secured.

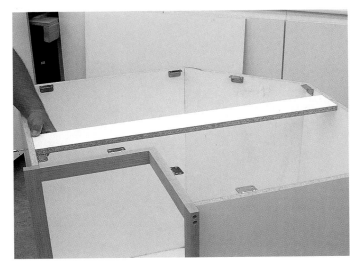

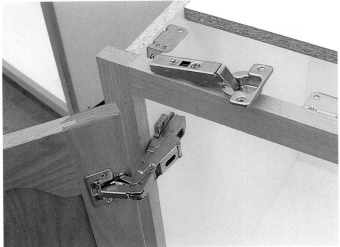

8 | A board must be installed across the center of the cabinet to support the lazy Susan bearing assembly. This upper support is nothing more than a piece of $^5/_8$"- or $^3/_4$"-thick melamine PB that's the same width as the baseboard. Secure it with two 2"-long screws through the cabinet side boards. If you have difficulty locating this board, wait until you're ready to install the lazy Susan upper bearing support and locate it directly over the bearing. This cabinet is now ready for the 32" lazy Susan and doors.

9 | The door sizes on this cabinet are special. The 1"-plus rule doesn't apply here, so we use a calculation of rail width minus $^1/_2$" for the doors. These two 10"-wide doors will have special hinges.

First, drill 35mm-diameter holes in one door, following the standard steps for hinge hole positioning. These cabinet doors require 170° hinges, but they cannot be installed with a $^1/_8$"-thick spacer. The wide-opening hinge plates are properly aligned on the cabinet sides by temporarily installing standard 100° to 120° hinges on the doors. Follow the hinge and door mounting steps using the standard-opening hinge. Once the plates are properly located, switch the standard-opening hinges with the 170°-wide hinges. They will be attached to the hinge plates already mounted on the cabinet sides.

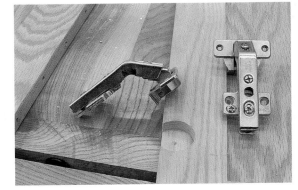

10 | One of the two doors that have 35mm-diameter holes for the wide hinges will also need hinge holes drilled on the opposite edge of the door for bifold hinges. These special hinges join the two doors. The holes for the bifold-type hinges are drilled so the center of the 35mm hole is 12.5mm from the door's edge. That position will create a $^3/_4$ hole in the door, which is required for these hinges.

11 | The installed doors require two 170°-opening hinges with standard mounting plates and two bifold-door hinges drilled as detailed in the previous step. Both hinge styles are adjustable, allowing you to accurately align these doors to the cabinet.

After installing the doors, follow the installation directions supplied with the lazy Susan assembly. Make sure it's properly positioned so the hinges don't bump against the revolving shelves or affect door operation. The cabinet is now ready to be installed.

BUILDING A DRAWER-OVER-DOOR BASE CABINET

The drawer-over-door base is a good way to gain extra drawer space. The cabinet shown in this illustration uses $5/8$"-thick sheet material; however, $3/4$" stock can be used by following the cutting list chart for standard base cabinet construction. In some kitchens many of the base cabinets are built in this style.

The large drawer in a 30" base unit is a useful addition to most kitchens. This cabinet style is also used when a counter cooktop is installed. In that circumstance, a false drawer front is permanently attached to hide the cooktop mechanism when the doors are opened. This cabinet style is also used for a sink cabinet, and the drawer face is often fitted with a flip-out kit and tray. The interior of the cabinet, behind the doors, can be fitted with either a pullout or an adjustable shelf.

DRAWER-OVER-DOOR BASE

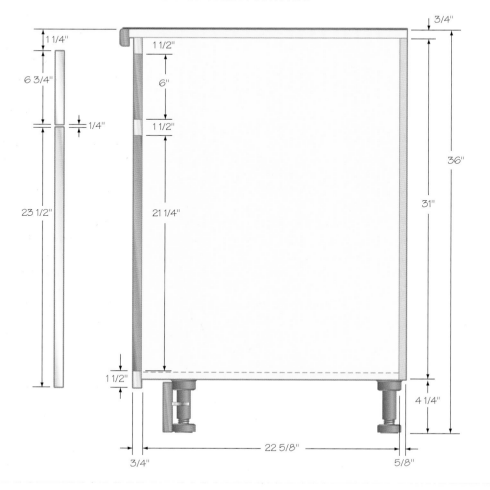

FOUR-DRAWER BASE CABINETS

The four-drawer base requires extra rails to fill the spaces between drawer faces.

Just about every kitchen has at least one of the four-drawer base cabinets. They are primarily used as a cutlery center and are often located near the sink, stove or dishwasher. The cabinet is nothing more than a standard base unit fitted with extra rails to hide the gaps between the drawers. As shown in the drawing on the next page, there are spacing and rail position considerations so that the $30^{1}/_{2}$" overall door, drawer/door or multiple-drawer height is maintained.

Construct the face frame using the dimensions as shown in the drawing on the next page. The five rails will divide the face frame into four drawer openings. The rails are 2" less in width than the outside face-frame dimension. Fasten each rail with glue and two 2" screws. Counterbore the screw holes so they can be filled with wood plugs if this cabinet is to be used as an end-of-run cabinet.

Using a 30" four-drawer base cabinet as an example, and standard $^{3}/_{4}$"-thick wood, this face frame would require

two stiles 1" wide by $31^{3}/_{4}$" long and five rails $1^{1}/_{2}$" wide by 28" long.

We don't have to be concerned about width as you can build any size drawer. You can use this cabinet to fill odd-size spaces in many situations. Apply the basic system design rule that inside face-frame width should equal inside carcass width, and make the cabinet any size you require. For example, if I had to fill a $26^{5}/_{8}$" space, I would construct a face frame with 1"-wide stiles and rail widths of $24^{5}/_{8}$". The carcass bottom board would be $24^{5}/_{8}$" wide, equaling the inside face-frame width. Remember, you don't have to be concerned with sizes, because you can make the drawer faces any width as long as they are 1" wider than the inside stile-to-stile dimension. All other carcass boards follow the standard rules: sides are 31" high by $22^{5}/_{8}$" wide (with $^{5}/_{8}$" sheet material) or $22^{1}/_{2}$" wide (with $^{3}/_{4}$"-thick sheet material). The bottom board is 2" narrower than the cabinet width, and the backboard is the total of the bottom board width and the two side thicknesses, by 31" high.

Drawer boxes, which will be detailed in chapter nine, are 1" less in height and 1" narrower than the drawer opening. Most of the drawer glides that are installed need a $^{1}/_{2}$" clearance on each side, and you should try to be as accurate as possible to achieve a proper fit.

Construction procedures for the drawer-over-door base cabinet are identical to the standard base cabinet, with an added $1^{1}/_{2}$"-high rail to cover the space between the door and drawer. The general design rule that applies is to maintain the $30^{1}/_{2}$" overall height so that we have the $1^{1}/_{4}$" reveal at the top of the face frame. As previously discussed, our standard door height is $30^{1}/_{2}$" for full-door cabinets. When we construct a drawer-over-door cabinet, or any other combination cabinet, we want to maintain that height so that all doors and drawers are at the same level. Maintaining this uniform line is visually pleasing, especially with base cabinets. The combination of a $23^{1}/_{2}$"-high door and a $6^{3}/_{4}$"-high drawer face plus the $^{1}/_{4}$" space between them gives us the required $30^{1}/_{2}$" height.

Drawer construction will be detailed in chapter nine using the $^{5}/_{8}$"- or $^{3}/_{4}$"-thick melamine PB box method, mounted on European bottom-mount drawer glides. Door installation is the same as with all other doors. If we use the 30" base cabinet as an example, we would require two doors $23^{1}/_{2}$" high by $14^{1}/_{2}$" wide. The drawer face would be $6^{3}/_{4}$" high by $29^{1}/_{16}$" wide. The drawer face width is a combination of the widths of the two doors, plus a gap allowance between the two doors of $^{1}/_{16}$".

In many of my kitchen projects, drawer faces are made from solid 1" × 8" hardwood. I decided on this method for a number of reasons, but primarily because 1" × 8" lumber is dressed to $^{3}/_{4}$" × $7^{1}/_{4}$", so you won't have to be concerned with edge-joining boards. This reduces the time and cost required to manufacture the cabinets. Cabinet door style will determine the amount of work necessary to produce a compatible drawer face. In most cases I use a router to form a roundover or cove detail to the drawer edge. This method will produce a drawer face for almost all of your applications.

Occasionally you may want a fancy and intricate drawer face. In those instances you can order or make a face to match your door style. However, the cost per drawer face increases and you may want to compare the costs, particularly if you have quite a few drawers in your kitchen.

FOUR-DRAWER BASE CABINET

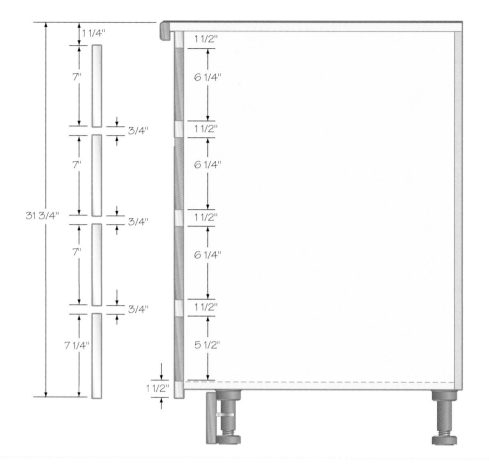

REDUCED- OR INCREASED-DEPTH BASE CABINETS

You may, on occasion, require base cabinets that are not standard 24"-deep units. One situation may be where you want a shallow cabinet base run for storage against a wall in a passageway. Or, on the other hand, you might want deeper cabinets for an island.

The easiest solution for a shallow version is to convert the standard upper cabinets into base cabinets by attaching adjustable legs. Sides and bottom boards can be cut wider for deeper cabinets without changing the dimensions of the backboard or face-frame members. As you may have already noticed, the overall cabinet height and door height are the same for the upper and base cabinets; only the depth is changed. You can purchase or build many different countertop sizes to accommodate these special base cabinets.

I have, on many occasions, used reduced-depth cabinets in a kitchen island situation. Space is sometimes a problem when designing islands, so I've often reduced the base units to a maximum of 18" deep and installed a 32"-wide island countertop. This allows the countertop to overhang the base cabinets by approximately 13", taking into account the door width and door side overhang. Stools can be used to provide a casual eating area, or as a place to sit while you're preparing food. The cabinet style in this system can be easily altered to meet any requirements.

SINK BASE CABINETS

Sink bases are standard drawer-over-door base cabinets, usually a 36" base, with a false drawer face or drawer face flip-out over the doors. The drawer face covers the bottom of the sink when the doors are open. I have built full-door sink bases to keep the cost down; however, my preference is a false drawer-over-door cabinet.

Install six legs on this cabinet, one at each corner as detailed earlier in this chapter, and one at the front and back in the middle of the base, to give it added support. This cabinet usually takes quite a bit of abuse because the supply and drain plumbing pipes must be installed. It's not uncommon to have someone crawling inside the cabinet to install and connect the service. It is also possible that you may have to relocate a cabinet leg if it ends up in the path of a plumbing pipe.

You may have to modify a shelf after you determine the location of the pipes inside the cabinet. Leave it until the installation is complete to determine where, if possible, you will be able to install the shelf. In many cases, shelf installation is not possible or practical because of the plumbing pipes.

chapter five

PANTRY AND MICROWAVE TALL CABINETS

FULL-HEIGHT PANTRY   FULL-HEIGHT MICROWAVE CABINET

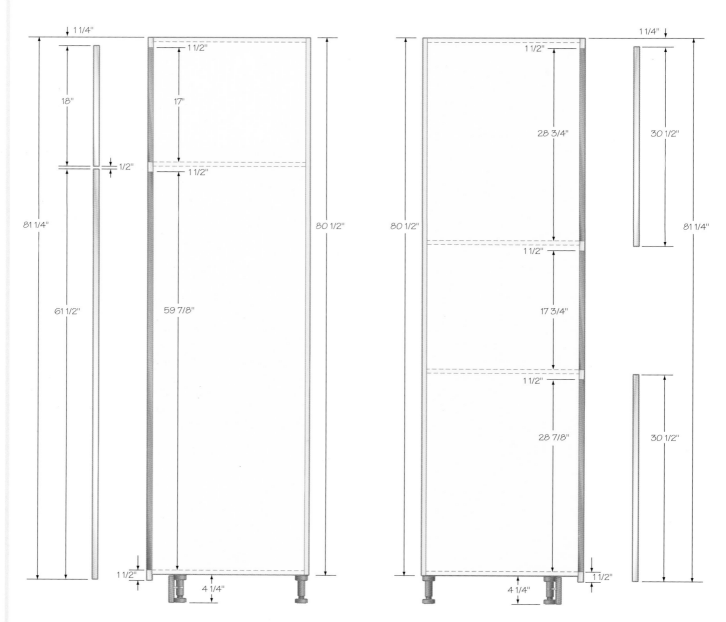

PANTRY CABINET

A pantry cabinet is simply an extended base cabinet with horizontal dividers.

Pantry and microwave cabinets share the same basic carcass assembly. The sides are $80\frac{1}{2}$" high and as deep as you require; the top and bottom shelves follow the width rules for standard cabinets; and the backboard is also $80\frac{1}{2}$" high and as wide as the bottom board plus the two side thicknesses. It may have one or two additional fixed shelves, depending on the style of the cabinet. The face frame is $81\frac{1}{4}$" high, following the rule that face frames are $\frac{3}{4}$" longer than cabinet sides, with 1"-wide stiles and $1\frac{1}{2}$"-wide top and bottom rails. The face frame may also contain up to five additional rails depending on the drawer and door combination. Each cabinet is normally fitted with adjustable shelves, drawers, pullouts or a combination of all three.

The upper section of the pantry cabinet is high and sometimes very deep. The tendency is to store kitchen utensils that are not often used for day-to-day meal preparation. To better use this space, you might consider installing vertical fixed partitions in place of the normal horizontal adjustable shelf. Vertical partitions allow you to store articles such as cutting boards, pizza trays and large serving platters that usually end up stacked on top of one another in a base cabinet. Simply attach the verticals with two screws through the top of the cabinet and two through the underside of the fixed shelf. You don't have to be concerned with shelf-loading capacity, as these verticals simply define cubicles for large item storage. Use $\frac{5}{8}$"- or $\frac{3}{4}$"-thick melamine-coated PB as the divider partitions, with plastic edge moulding, veneer tape or hardwood edging covering the cut end.

The drawing on the previous page details the construction of a pantry cabinet in which you install adjustable shelves or pullouts. The pantry cabinet is built using two doors, with the lower, larger door having three European hinges installed. The lower door is usually $61\frac{1}{2}$" high and the upper door is 18" high. A $\frac{1}{2}$" gap is left between the upper and lower door so that we maintain the $1\frac{1}{4}$" space at the top of the face frame. A rail is installed, with a fixed shelf board, at the point where the upper and lower doors meet.

MICROWAVE CABINET

This cabinet is a combination base and upper cabinet with a fixed shelf compartment for the microwave oven.

Microwave cabinets, as shown in the drawing on the previous page, follow all the standard cabinet construction principles and usually contain a lower drawer bank or pullouts behind doors, with adjustable shelves behind the upper doors. The middle opening normally contains the microwave. The opening space is large enough for most microwaves using a standard cabinet width of 27", which has a 25" inside face-frame width. When planning for a microwave cabinet as part of the renovation project, don't forget to have an electrician wire an outlet in the space where the microwave is to be installed.

If you are going to install four drawers in the base of this cabinet, follow the same rules and dimensions that apply to a four-drawer base cabinet. Remember to use spacing cleats, as detailed in chapter nine, if you are installing pullouts behind the doors on either cabinet. The upper sections of these cabinets are normally fitted with adjustable shelves.

The microwave cabinet carcass can be built using wood-veneer-covered particleboard, as a portion of the cabinet interior is visible. A $\frac{5}{8}$"- or $\frac{3}{4}$"-thick wood-veneer board will allow the face frame to extend beyond the carcass, which makes it easy to use the wood doorstop moulding around the perimeter that is visible. This technique covers screws and softens the look of these large cabinets. Check the moulding thickness before cutting your tall cabinet stiles.

Microwave and pantry cabinets are simply an upper cabinet and a lower cabinet with the space between them connected. Install these cabinets before or at the same time as the base cabinets so your maximum cabinet height is defined. This uniformity of height is important for upper cabinet trim installation, as well as visual appearance. Since these cabinets are often end-of-run units, finishing trim should be applied, which will be detailed in a later chapter.

Don't let the size or apparent complexity of these cabinets bother you. They are simple to build although somewhat awkward to handle alone. You will probably need someone's assistance during the assembly stage.

The backboards of these cabinets, like all the other standard units, will be installed over the side edges, which reveals the backboard edge at the side of the cabinet. These visible edges will be trimmed with doorstop moulding to finish the cabinet after installation.

Finally, visualize these tall cabinets as uppers and lowers with common full-height sides. Cut the horizontal shelves to the width you require for a microwave, built-in oven or any other special application. If you keep the general principle of face-frame height at $\frac{3}{4}$" longer than the cabinet sides, you can easily design and construct any tall cabinet.

SPECIAL TRIM, ACCESSORIES AND CUSTOM CABINETS

FINISHING END CABINETS

Base and upper cabinets that are at the end of a run, and open to view on one side, must be finished so the melamine PB sides can't be seen. Identify these cabinets in the planning stage.

To allow for the finishing trim that's used on end-of-run cabinets, increase the stile width by $\frac{1}{4}$" for $\frac{5}{8}$" material or $\frac{3}{8}$" for $\frac{3}{4}$" material on the side to be finished. This stile width increase technique is needed for end finishing, contour fitting of the cabinet to a wall or custom cabinet fitting of a cabinet run that is closed by walls on both ends. In the planning stage I normally label a cabinet that requires increased stile width with a measurement and side designation. For example, a 30" cabinet that will be used as a left-side end-of-run cabinet will be shown on my plan as a "30" plus $\frac{1}{4}$" L" upper or base.

Standard stile width is 1", and standard side thickness can be either $\frac{5}{8}$" or $\frac{3}{4}$". This means, on a normal cabinet, the stile extends beyond the side by $\frac{3}{8}$" with $\frac{5}{8}$" material, and $\frac{1}{4}$" when using $\frac{3}{4}$"-thick sheet stock. The $\frac{1}{4}$" or $\frac{3}{8}$" increase in stile width makes the stile extend a total of $\frac{5}{8}$" past the side.

After cabinet installation I install $\frac{1}{4}$"-thick veneer plywood to match the doors, and wood doorstop moulding, which is slightly thicker than $\frac{1}{4}$", around the perimeter of the cabinet end.

construction tip

Apply $\frac{1}{4}$" veneer-covered plywood with construction cement and brad nails to the exposed end of the cabinet. On base cabinets I add a $\frac{3}{4}$" filler to the bottom of the cabinet side to extend it to $31\frac{3}{4}$", so the applied veneer panel will be flush with the bottom of the face frame.

The screw holes that secure the end-of-run cabinet stile to the cabinet rails must be filled with wood plugs so they won't be visible. I use a $\frac{1}{8}$" countersink drill bit assembly with a $\frac{3}{8}$" counterbore hole for these screws. I fill the holes with $\frac{3}{8}$" wood plugs sanded flush to finish the visible stile sides.

FINISHING UNDER UPPER CABINETS

Some cabinetmakers leave the underside of upper cabinets unfinished. This area, although not normally visible when standing in front of the cabinets, may be seen by someone sitting in the kitchen. I believe finishing this area adds a measure of quality to the cabinet work.

Install $\frac{1}{4}$" veneer plywood of the same wood type as the doors, cut to fit, on the underside of the uppers. The front edge of the veneer will not be visible because the face frame extends $\frac{3}{4}$" below the cabinet carcass. For an end-of-run cabinet, the end edge of the veneer plywood can be hidden by the doorstop moulding used to finish the side.

Secure the veneer plywood panels with small brad nails or contact cement. The small nails won't be seen, and the nail head holes can be easily filled with a colored putty.

CUSTOM CABINETS

Special needs often require a custom cabinet. The primary user of the kitchen may want a cabinet for unique cooking utensils, crafts or other appliances. Designing and building that unique cabinet is a common task in many custom kitchens.

Most custom cabinets are simply a modification to the standard base and upper units. Analyze the requirements and apply the same construction principles used to build the standard carcasses.

UNDERCABINET LIGHTING

Undercabinet lighting is a common accessory in many kitchen renovation projects. Numerous types and styles of lighting assemblies are available, including low-voltage and fluorescent fixtures.

I used a fluorescent lamp assembly with this cabinet system, mainly because of the energy efficiency of this type of light, as well as its low heat properties.

It's best to decide whether you want undercabinet lighting during the planning stage, because power and switches must be installed. The undercabinet lighting system consists of a 1×4 board mounted on edge under the upper cabinets, approximately 6" from the wall. Use angle brackets to secure this board under the cabinets. Mount the fluorescent fixture, which is available in 2', 3' and 4' lengths, to the back of the board.

GENERAL LIGHTING

Custom light fixtures tend to be expensive, but proper lighting is an important requirement in the kitchen. You can build your own fixture for less than half the cost of similar units on the market.

The wood-enclosed assembly in the photo contains a 4' fluorescent fixture. The lamps illuminate a large area, and they don't generate a great deal of heat. I have two of these fixtures in my kitchen, and they work well.

The boxes are 1×6 hardwood lumber assembled using a butt joint on each corner. I secured the box with glue and wood screws. The underside of the fixture is trimmed with a wood doorstop moulding, and a sheet of transparent acrylic plastic rests on the lip of the moulding.

You may have to route wiring in the frame, so leave a little extra room. This is a simple and cost-effective way to get high-quality lighting in your new kitchen.

REFRIGERATOR SURROUND CABINETS

Refrigerator surround cabinets are a modified version of the 33" over-the-fridge cabinet. Extend the sides and stiles to meet your overall height requirement, normally the same height as the top of your upper cabinet position, using wood-veneer PB and

hardwood stiles. I extend the stile on the panel side from the floor to the top of the cabinet. The depth of an over-the-fridge cabinet must be increased to fully enclose the fridge. The cabinet width should also be increased to maintain the inside clearance for the fridge. In most cases, you can use the normal 1"-wide stiles, but verify that you'll have enough outside overhang to hide the edges of the perimeter trim moulding you plan to use.

Modify how you fasten the top and bottom boards with the use of screws and brackets. If you plan to use wood doorstop moulding as a perimeter trim, place the screws that support the bottom and top boards in areas where they will be hidden by the trim. Reduce the depth of the top and bottom boards by $5/8$" so the backboard is set inside and flush with the back edges of the sides in the rear of the cabinet.

REFRIGERATOR PANELS

Many modern refrigerators will accept either $1/4$"-thick veneer plywood panels or raised solid-wood panels. The appliance has a mounting kit or the option can be purchased.

These panels are the same as the center section of your cabinet doors. They can be finished to match the doors and add a built-in, custom look to your kitchen project. The wood panel feature is also available with some dishwashers. The installation of appliance panels is quick and easy using the manufacturer's kits.

CUSTOM STOVES AND RANGE HOODS

Slide-in stoves and custom range hoods have become popular in the last few years. The stove fits tightly into a measured space between cabinets and a countertop that has been cut to an exact size. The manufacturer will provide you with the cabinet-to-cabinet measurement for the slide-in stove.

Typically, the countertop is installed over the space and a notch is cut to accept the stove. The cutout dimensions are exact, and in my experience of installing these slide-in stoves, there's no room for error. The stovetop has a small lip that overlaps the countertop, but it's often only $1/8$" to $1/4$", so accurate cutting of the countertop is important.

Custom range hoods are available in many styles, including slim-line, low-profile and slide-out models. Another option is a combination range hood and microwave. They are normally 30" wide, but often require specific clearances above the stove elements and special mounting procedures.

MICROWAVE CABINETS

Space is often an issue, and getting the microwave off the countertop can free up valuable working areas. But a tall microwave cabinet isn't always a practical option for your new kitchen.

Microwaves can be installed under upper cabinets, and placed at the same level as the bottom of standard-height cabinets by building a reduced-height upper. I normally build a box that's open on the front and back to hold the appliance. The bottom board of the box is sometimes extended for large ovens.

SINK FLIP-OUTS

Sink cabinets, normally a 36" standard base, are not usually fitted with $30\frac{1}{2}$" full cabinet-height doors. They are built as a drawer-over-door cabinet so that the underside of the sink is not visible when the cabinet doors are open.

Because the sink occupies the space needed for the drawer carcass, the drawer is a false face and nonoperational. Normally this space is lost. But various suppliers, such as Rev-A-Shelf, sell a flip-out kit that includes hinges and a plastic tray. You can install this kit on the false drawer front and have a functional flip-out drawer face with a plastic tray inside, used to store scrubbing pads and dish soap. Your local kitchen hardware supply outlet should stock these kits.

UPPER CABINET TRIM

The face-frame upper cabinet design, using a $30\frac{1}{2}$"-tall door, leaves a $1\frac{1}{4}$" space on the face frame above the door. That section can be used to install a wide variety of mouldings.

High crown moulding or a low-profile moulding, similar to a chair rail, visually enhances your project. Experiment with a few styles after the cabinets have been installed.

The mouldings can be nailed to the face frame and mitered at the corners. Some of the moulding styles, such as 4" crown, can be difficult to install, particularly at the mitered corners. A power miter saw and attention to detail will usually result in perfect joints. Remember the upside down and backwards rule when mitering crown moulding: Imagine the saw table as the ceiling and the backstop as the wall when cutting, making sure the top of your moulding is resting on the saw table, and the miters will be exact.

I use solid wood that matches the doors and face frames. The box is attached to the underside of a reduced-height upper with screws or nuts and bolts. The back of the box is purposely left open to accommodate the electrical plug installed for the oven.

RAISED UPPER CABINETS

Raising one of the units can visually enhance the upper cabinet line. This works best where a break or change in direction occurs. The 24" angled upper corner is an ideal cabinet to raise 6" higher than the adjoining units. You can also add interest when you fit this cabinet with a glass door and shelves. However, glass door carcasses are made with a veneer particleboard because you can see the cabinet interior. Usually the veneer PB for this cabinet matches the door and face-frame wood.

I've also raised over-the-stove cabinets, which created an interesting look. This cabinet is normally reduced in height and not very practical for storage purposes. Increasing the height by 6" above the cabinet line looks great and enlarges the interior space.

KITCHEN WORK CENTERS

Desks and writing areas are often needed in the modern kitchen. Computers are often a part of the equipment in today's kitchens and require a work area.

Desktops are 30" high and made using standard cabinets that have been modified. Use reduced-height base units, including drawer banks, and attach any style of countertop. The wood-edged top detailed in chapter eight is perfect for this application.

Use the rule of 12s when calculating seating height for these work areas: The chair or stool should be 12" lower than the work surface for maximum comfort.

DISPLAY SHELVES

Display shelving for collectibles is often part of a kitchen project. Many people have favorite items to display, and open kitchen shelving is the perfect spot. There's always an extra 6" or 8" of wall space that's too small for a cabinet, but ideally suited for an open shelf.

These open shelves serve many useful purposes; they add visual interest to your cabinetry, provide a display area and allow the cabinetmaker to custom fit a complete run of cabinets on any wall. The shelves can be made to fit any space.

Normally I use solid wood for these display shelves. I've built half-round shelves, angled units and simple, straight, open shelving between cabinets for books. Your imagination is the only limiting factor with these display cabinets.

construction tip

The possibilities available to the woodworker to design and build kitchen accessories are unlimited. I've seen pegboard, mounted on 1" dowels, installed on the inside of cabinet doors for storing pot lids. A unique spice rack made with 1×4 wood at either end, and $1/2$" dowels spaced 1" on center to hold spice bottles in a drawer. And base pullouts of every shape and size to accommodate special needs.

I suggest you look through magazines and browse the accessories section of the home building supply centers, where you'll find many items that can be built inexpensively in your workshop.

BUILDING ISLANDS AND PENINSULAS

PENINSULA WITH SEATING

Seating at an island or peninsula that has an overhang usually means using stools or high bar-style chairs. Seat height is determined using the rule of 12s, which is a relationship of countertop to chair height. The standard 30"-high desk needs an 18"-high chair. An overhanging countertop that is 36" high requires a stool with a seat height of 24". Simply stated, the seat height should be 12" lower than the work-surface height for maximum comfort.

PENINSULA WITHOUT SEATING

Standard cabinet depth and width can be modified to build islands and peninsulas. Islands without seating can be standard- or increased-depth base cabinets. However, always calculate the total depth adding the doors, overhangs and finish trim on the rear of the cabinets. The ends of the island are finished because they are exposed, so remember to account for the extra width when determining countertop measurements.

I normally don't use adjustable legs for island or peninsula cabinet bases, because the cabinets must be anchored to the floor. Construct a base platform using $^{3}/_{4}$" plywood or construction-grade $1^{1}/_{2}$"-thick lumber that's $4^{1}/_{4}$" high. Face the platform with $4^{1}/_{4}$"-high hardwood that matches the door and face-frame wood as the finished kick plate. The base frame, with finished face, should be 3" to $3^{1}/_{2}$" in from all cabinet edges that are open.

Locate the platform on the floor and level if necessary. Use brackets to secure it to the floor. Anchor the cabinets through the bottom board to the platform using screws. The exposed heads of the screws can be covered with caps.

Traffic patterns and safety are a concern when designing islands and peninsulas. Kitchen islands may be freestanding units or placed against a wall, more properly called a peninsula, and often define traffic patterns in the room. For this reason, countertop edges should be designed and constructed to minimize accidents, particularly with small children. Order your island countertops with radius edges or build a custom countertop with mitered corners (see chapter eight). Always account for the loss in length because of these eased or radius ends when calculating your requirements.

Islands must be finished on all four sides and peninsulas require finished surfaces on three sides. The doors and face frame are on one side, and the exposed melamine PB carcass is usually covered with $^{1}/_{4}$"-thick veneer plywood.

The perimeter of these covered sides can be trimmed with doorstop moulding with a right-angle trim piece on the corners. It's necessary to widen the stiles by $^{1}/_{4}$", making the overhang on the carcass sides larger to accommodate the thickness of plywood and perimeter trim.

Island and peninsula backs can be finished with $^{1}/_{4}$" veneer plywood and a flat trim around the perimeter of the cabinet. You can choose from dozens of trim options and styles to make these large surfaces interesting.

Changing the depth of base cabinets for an island work center is not a diffi-cult process. The only carcass components that are altered are the depths of the sides and bottom board. All other dimensions remain constant in the standard cabinet.

The same holds true for increased-depth cabinets. These minor changes to meet custom requirements show the flexibility of this building system. You should be able to make changes to any of the standard cabinet dimensions to meet all of your needs.

Kitchen islands, whether fixed, peninsula or movable, give you an opportunity to design some unique and useful features in a kitchen. They can increase the counter space in a small kitchen and add a bit of flair to a large area. Often, I use the island and peninsula concept as area dividers to help define the kitchen space while maintaining the open feeling that most people desire in today's kitchens.

White melamine PB covered with $\frac{1}{4}$" veneer plywood isn't the only sheet material combination that can be used to build islands and peninsulas. Cabinets can be constructed using $\frac{5}{8}$"- or $\frac{3}{4}$"-thick veneer-covered plywoods or particleboards. Both faces are covered with veneer that matches the cabinet doors and face frames, so all that's required is a little trim around the perimeter.

MOBILE ISLANDS

Kitchen islands that can be moved, sometimes called portable work centers, are another option that increases the functionality of a kitchen. Additional workspace is often required to meet meal preparation demands.

Any base cabinet can be adapted for use as a mobile island with a few modi-fications. For instance, if you want a movable island, construct a standard base unit without the legs. To strength-en the bottom board, attach pieces of $\frac{3}{4}$" wood, about 4" square, on all four corners of the cabinet. Make certain the wood fully covers the bottom edge of the cabinet side, so the wheel will properly support it. The overhang of the face frame will hide the front edges of the wood supports. The sides and back can have $\frac{1}{4}$" plywood veneer installed.

Attach four wheel assemblies to the bottom of the cabinet. Build the cabinet with $1\frac{1}{4}$"-wide stiles on the face frame,

in place of the standard 1"-wide stiles, so you can install veneer plywood and doorstop moulding as the finish trim. The back of the cabinet can be finished in the same manner. Buy or build a countertop that overhangs the cabinet on all edges. Angle brackets will secure the countertop to the cabinet. You can also install one of the latest solid-surface countertop materials or even a granite slab, which will give you a beautiful and unique island.

The interior of the island cabinet can be designed in many ways. A standard drawer-over-door base will give you a useful place to put cutting utensils and other equipment. A full-door standard cabinet can be fitted with multiple adjustable shelves for storage. Vertical fixed shelving is another option if the island will be used to store cutting boards and large trays.

chapter eight

COUNTERTOPS

CONVENTIONAL ROLLTOP COUNTERTOPS

The simplest and least expensive approach in a renovation project is to use one of the many styles of roll or postformed laminate countertops that are readily available. Laminate is applied under pressure over a particle-board form that has a curved, moulded backsplash and front edge. It is relatively inexpensive and available at one of the many countertop specialty companies in most major cities.

If you're building a great deal of custom cabinetry, you might have some problems with postformed tops, as they are fairly standard in size and design. However, this style can be used for the majority of projects.

Postformed countertops are usually sold by the running foot. You can get bartop countertops, island tops and preassembled or assemble-yourself angled tops. Most countertop suppliers will cut and assemble right-angle countertops, including ones that go from a standard countertop to a bartop on a peninsula.

If possible, have the supplier assemble the right-angle runs, as they seem to produce a better joint in their shop than can be achieved on the job site. Suppliers have roll countertop designs called bullnose, flat-top, traditional, etc., and countertop styles such as bartop, regular and island. Finish materials are numerous and varied from manufacturers such as Wilsonart, Formica and Arborite. Costs are reasonable and they can supply countertops for most of your needs.

COUNTERTOP MATERIAL OPTIONS

SOLID-SURFACE MATERIALS

A popular material is the so-called solid-surface countertop, with product names such as Corian and Gibraltar. This can be an expensive alternative, and specialists trained by the manufacturers normally do installation. Not everyone can afford the luxury of this material, but you may find it fits within your budget. The demand seems to be increasing, and the cost is getting lower as more manufacturers enter the marketplace. Contact two or three of your local countertop suppliers and speak to them about their pricing schedule, product supply, sample material and literature.

CERAMIC TILE

Ceramic tile is used as a countertop material in some kitchen renovation projects. It is one of the oldest and most versatile materials. Available in many sizes, shapes and styles, this long-lasting and durable product can lend itself to many design applications. Ceramic tile is stain resistant and heat-proof. However, the grout lines require constant maintenance due to the possibility of staining from food. It's best to seal the grout with a high-quality silicone sealer prior to use.

Ceramics are often used on the wall

between the upper and lower cabinets because they are easy to clean. Application on the walls is a straightforward process and fairly simple as there are normally only three or four rows of tile to apply. Information on wall tile application is available at most tile specialty stores and is quite often a do-it-yourself procedure.

Countertop ceramic tile installation is also a relatively simple operation that requires a bit of skill and a lot of patience. Tile application over water-resistant plywood seems to work well with the proper glue and grout. Again, ask the experts at the tile center for the right combination with the product you purchase. Choose the tile, but remember to calculate the width of tiles and tile spacing before cutting your plywood

to the correct size. With this method you can avoid a lot of unnecessary tile cutting. Band the countertop edge, following tile installation, with a 1" × 2" hardwood strip to match the wood on your cabinets for a professional-looking finish. If you want to avoid a wood edge, you can purchase special edge tiles with a raised lip to complete the installation.

GRANITE

Natural materials such as granite, as shown in the photo, are becoming popular. The cost is toward the high end, often in the same range as solid-surface materials. It is a beautiful and long-lasting countertop option that you might want to investigate.

Granite is available in many colors, but not in as wide a range as the high-pressure laminates. The colors are natural, so you'll notice some variance in long runs, and from section to section, if your kitchen has a number of countertop runs.

Stone is normally installed by specialists because of the training and tools that are required. Diamond cutting blades and heavy-duty polishing equipment are just a couple of the specialty tools required. Surprisingly, stone can break or be easily damaged if not installed properly, so the work is best left in the hands of professionals.

Building Custom Wood-Edged Countertops

This countertop style is easily made and well within any woodworker's capabilities. The process involves attaching a wood edge trim to a panel, called the substrate, and covering the top with a high-pressure laminate.

These laminates are made with decorative surface papers impregnated with melamine resins, which are pressed over kraft paper core sheets. These sheets are then bonded at pressures of 1,000 pounds or more per square inch, with temperatures approaching 300° F (149° C). The finished sheets are trimmed, and the backs are sanded to facilitate bonding. Most manufacturers have many patterns available.

High-pressure laminate materials come in two thicknesses. The thinner version is used to manufacture post-formed countertops that are common in almost every kitchen and bathroom. The thicker, general-purpose (GP) laminates are used for applications like the top in the photo at right. The GP material is able to stand more abuse because of its thickness.

This great-looking wood-edged countertop style has a number of uses. It can be used as a kitchen or bathroom top, a work center/desk or as a utility countertop. I've used it in dozens of projects over the years. And, because the laminate is available in 4' × 8' or

5' × 12' sheets, most tops can be made without a seam.

You can use any stable sheet material as the substrate, including particleboard, plywood or medium-density fiberboard. I recommend a minimum $^3/_4$"-thick substrate for strength and stability. The wood edge can be any hardwood or softwood that complements your cabinets.

1 | Cut the substrate sheet material to the required size. Reduce the desired finished size by ³/₄" where a wood edge will be installed. I am using ³/₄"-thick particleboard as my substrate for this top.

2 | Attach the wood edge with glue and screws covered by wood plugs. You can also use dowels or biscuits. Any of these three options will work equally well. Be sure the top of the wood edge and the surface of the substrate are perfectly flush. If not, sand both to achieve a flat, smooth surface. This is a critical step, as the laminate won't bind properly to an uneven surface.

3 | Cut the laminate 1" longer than the substrate on all edges. That extra width and length will allow for any slight positioning errors.

Apply a contact adhesive to both the underside of the laminate and the substrate top. Make certain there's an even coat on both surfaces, and that all areas are covered.

Many types of contact cement are available. I'm using a roller-grade liquid, but brush and spray contact cements are available at most home stores.

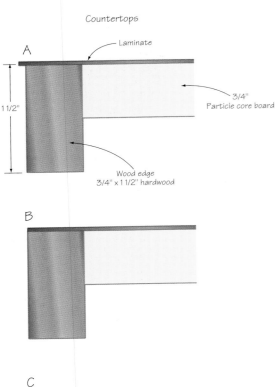

Countertops

A
Laminate
1 1/2"
3/4"
Particle core board
Wood edge
3/4" x 1 1/2" hardwood

B

C

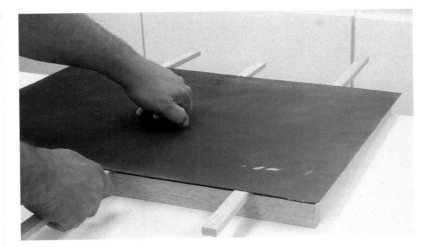

4 | The contact cement is set when it's dry to the touch. Read the instructions listed on your container for best results. This adhesive will bond only to another surface with the same glue applied. Therefore, place dry sticks on the substrate to keep the materials from touching until the laminate is correctly positioned. Be careful: Once the two glued surfaces touch, they are bonded!

Remove the center stick and press the laminate in place with your hand. Move your hand from the center to the outside edges pushing out any trapped air bubbles. A pressure roller is the best tool to use to make certain the laminate is completely bonded to the substrate. If you don't have a commercial roller, use a wooden rolling pin or large wood dowel. Again, roll from the center to the edges, paying particular attention to the laminate edges.

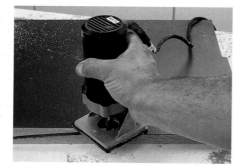

5 The excess laminate can be cut flush to the wood edge using a flush-trim router bit. These bits have a guide bearing that tracks along the substrate and wood edges, cutting the laminate flush.

I'm using a small trim router; however, these trim bits will work fine in any router. Always verify that the bit is clean and the bearing is in good shape.

6 Use a roundover bit in a router to make a simple rounded profile on the bottom of the wood edge.

Cut the top or laminated surface of the countertop using the same roundover bit. Set the bit so its straight cutters, which are above the curved portion of the bit, cut slightly lower than the thickness of the laminate material. That cutting pass will trim the laminate cleanly and expose the wood under the laminate, as well as rounding over the top edge.

7 The wood edge and laminate profile should look like the end view shown in this photograph. Once the all the cutting has been completed, sand the wood edge smooth and apply a finish.

ANGLED OR ROUNDED COUNTERTOP CORNERS

If you have children running around, or desire a softer look, the substrate can be angle-cut, fitted with 1" × 2" wood banding and sanded round prior to laminate installation and routering.

The edge trim and roundover bits will follow the wood-edged profile and cut the laminate to almost any shape. The wood-edged tops can be cut into many shapes to meet your requirements. It's a flexible style of top that's easily customized.

ISLAND COUNTERTOPS

Island countertops have four exposed counter edges and are usually a custom width. These top styles can be ordered from the supplier, or you can use the custom wood-edge style.

Bartop, island and peninsula cabinet systems are becoming more and more popular as people tear down walls to create open-concept homes. Base cabinets with fancy tops are created as room dividers, providing workspace but maintaining an open feeling.

Many of my new kitchen projects use the island and peninsula concept to add excitement to newly created spaces, simply by removing a wall.

BARTOPS

Bartops are nothing more than wide countertops that are finished on the front and back edge. They can be ordered from any countertop supplier, or you can make a custom wood-edged countertop. Simply follow the method for the custom countertop style and finish all exposed edges with hardwood. Normally, bartops butt against a wall at one end, so you don't need to finish that end with a wood edge.

Using general-purpose laminate, which is a thicker material, will provide you with a durable countertop. However, use care when cutting to avoid damaging the laminate. The best router bits are carbide tipped and work exceptionally well for this application.

The wood edge in my case was oak, but any species can be used. Stick with the major brands of laminate material for the best results. High-quality material and contact cement will give you perfect results every time.

Some of the adhesives are toxic, particularly the petroleum-based products, so work in a well-vented area. And make sure you closely follow the application directions from the adhesive manufacturer, because heat range and humidity levels are important when using these products.

INSTALLING A BACKSPLASH

Backsplash material is normally 1×3 hardwood of the same type as the cabinet wood. Attach the backsplash material to the wall with screws in countersunk holes. Cover the holes with wooden buttons, or attach the wood edge to the top with $1\frac{1}{2}$" screws, from the underside, before the countertop is installed. It's also good practice to run a bead of clear silicone between the wood backsplash and laminate to seal the joint.

MAKING CABINET DOORS AND DRAWERS

FLAT PANEL DOORS

These doors can be made with any sheet material, not just veneer boards. Consider melamine particleboard in any of the dozens of colors available, edged with matching tape. Veneer plywoods and particleboards, as detailed in the following steps, make a great-looking door with some accent moulding applied. Medium-density fiberboard (MDF) is another great alternative when you want a low-cost door that can be routed and painted.

1 Slab or flat-panel doors are made from sheet goods or glued-up wood panels. They are an option when a number of low-cost doors is required.

Utility and storage cabinets don't often require fancy doors, so the slab door is the answer. But don't sell them short; many kitchens, including my own, have veneer-covered particleboard doors, which is one of the popular slab-style doors.

One 32-square-foot sheet of melamine or veneer-covered particleboard will yield quite a few doors. If you have a kitchen, bathroom, laundry or storage room project on hold because you can't afford to make solid-wood raised-panel doors, take a look at this low-cost solution.

Preglued, heat-sensitive wood veneer is available in all types and sizes to match the veneered sheet goods you choose. Cut the door to size and apply the edge tape.

2 Commercial trimmers and chisels used to trim the wood-veneer tape tend to follow the grain and rip the edges. I use a flush-trim bit in my router, being careful to hold the tool tight to the board edge so I won't nick the veneer.

Lightly sand the edges with fine paper after you've completed trimming the tape. The ends can be dressed square with a file.

3 You can add interest and design to these flat doors by using commercial mouldings to create a pattern. The moulding is attached to the door with glue and brad nails.

construction tip

Cut the tenons slightly thicker than necessary. Test the fit by gently pushing the tenons into their mortises. Sand or file the tenons carefully until you achieve a snug fit.

If you're doing a number of doors, have all the rails ready for tenon cutting at the same time. Test the saw setup until you get a good fit, then cut all the rails. This procedure saves saw setup time, and all the joints will be perfect.

Frame and Panel Doors

Frame and panel doors are loosely broken up into two categories. The first are doors made with $1/4$"-thick veneer plywood, and the second group has solid-wood center panels.

Many woodworkers feel that frame and panel door making is difficult. However, just the opposite is true; it is an easy process. Frame and panel doors are commonly made using vertical frame members called stiles and horizontal frame members call rails. Two $3/4$"-thick by $2 1/4$"-wide stiles and two $3/4$"-thick by $2 1/4$"-wide rails, are required to build the frame. The center panel can be plywood, solid wood or glass.

The sample project door will have a finished size of 14" wide and 24" high. The door frame is made using $3/4$"-thick stock, and the panel is $1/4$" veneer plywood.

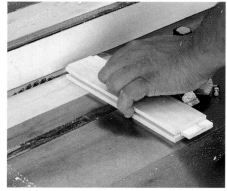

1 Cut two stiles $2 1/4$" wide by 24" long. The rails are $2 1/4$" wide by $10 1/2$" long. Rail length is equal to the total width of the door minus the width of two stiles, or $9 1/2$" long. We have to add the length of two tenons, which are each $1/2$" long, to the rail length. The rail-length formula is door width minus the width of two stiles, plus the length of two tenons. For example, the same style door that's 20" wide would have $16 1/2$"-long rails ($20" - 4 1/2" + 1" = 16 1/2"$).

Form a groove, centered on the inside edge of each stile and rail, that's $1/4$" wide by $1/2$" deep. Use a table saw or slot-cutter bit and center the groove on each edge.

2 On both ends of the two rails, cut a tenon that is $1/4$" thick by $1/2$" long. Make certain the tenon is centered on the rail. These tenons are easily formed using a table saw.

Both solid center panel options use a solid-wood panel. Edge-glue wood strips using biscuits to create a blank panel. There should be a $1/16$" gap between the panel and groove bottom on all four edges, as discussed earlier.

Cope-and-Stick Doors

Cope and stick is a joinery method using special router bits to cut profiles in the stiles and rails of a frame door. The bit sets consist of a cope bit and a stick bit. Some companies offer a combination bit that will cut both profiles when the blades are rearranged, but I prefer the two-bit set. A third bit, called a panel-raising bit, is necessary when you are making raised-panel doors.

The stick bit cuts a mortise on the inside edge of each frame member. It also profiles a decorative pattern. The cope bit is used to cut a mirror-image profile of that pattern, as well as a tenon on the ends of each rail. These are expensive bit sets but well worth the money if you plan to make your own doors. A good bit set will produce a high-quality joint, so look for well-made carbide sets.

Each cope-and-stick bit set cuts a little differently. Final door width is dependent on how much material is removed by the bits. For example, I

tested my set and determined that my rail width, after cutting the stile and rail profiles, needs to be cut $3\frac{3}{8}$" shorter than my desired final door width. That is based on building the door with $2\frac{1}{4}$"-wide stiles.

If I needed a 16"-wide door, I would cut my rails $12\frac{5}{8}$" wide. Test your own set and determine a rough-cut width for the rails. You should be able to determine the characteristics of the set you're using and produce any door width needed.

1 Profile the inside edge of each stile and rail with the stick bit. A router that's at least 2 horsepower (hp), mounted in a table, will cut the edges properly and safely.

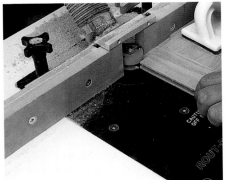

2 The cope bit is used to profile both ends of the two rails. Align the cope bit using a previously cut stick profile. Test the cut and fit with a scrap piece of $\frac{3}{4}$"-thick wood.

3 Dry fit the rails and stiles to ensure a proper fit. The joints should be snug, but not too tight. Once the frame has been tested, cut the raised panel.

VENEER PLYWOOD CENTER PANEL

The simplest center panel for these doors is a $\frac{1}{4}$"-thick sheet of veneer plywood to match your cabinets. Cut the panel to the inside frame dimension plus $\frac{7}{16}$" more on the ends and sides to fit in the grooves. The result will be a panel that's $\frac{1}{8}$" narrower than the top-to-bottom and side-to-side groove

measurement to allow room for expansion and contraction. This space is not critical when using $\frac{1}{4}$" plywood, but very important when solid-wood panels are installed. Assemble the door using glue on the tenons only. Do not glue the panel as it must float freely to account for expansion and contraction during humidity-level changes.

SOLID-WOOD CENTER PANEL

Two table saw options are available if you want to make a solid, raised center panel. Be careful when using either option, as you are normally dealing with a large panel that can be awkward to cut.

Solid-Wood Option #1

 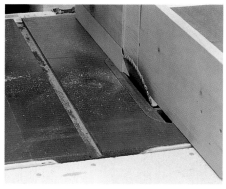 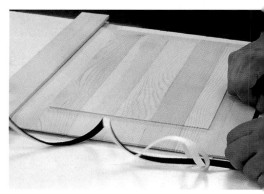

1 Use the table saw to cut $^1/_8$"-deep grooves on the panel face. All four edges of the panel are guided along the fence, cutting the panel 2" from each edge.

2 Tip the saw blade 10° away from the fence. I have extended the height of my fence to give better control when cutting high panels. It's a nice feature and can be easily made with a few boards.

Set the fence to cut a $^3/_{16}$" edge on the door. That will give the correct taper and the panel will sit in the frame grooves. Cut all four edges, setting the saw blade to the height of the four grooves scored on the panel face.

3 Sand the raised section of your panel with a large flat sanding block. Assemble the door using glue on the tenons only. Do not glue the panel. Before inserting the panel, place small pieces of weather-strip foam in the grooves to stop any door rattles.

Solid-Wood Option # 2

1 Use the table saw miter gauge to attach a board on the saw at right angles to the blade. The board can be clamped or attached with screws. The straight edge of the board should be crossing the center of the blade when it's just below the table surface.

2 Turn on the saw and raise the blade $^1/_{32}$". Push the panel blank across the blade, cutting all four edges, starting with the top and bottom of the panel. Raise the blade by $^1/_{32}$" on each pass. Take it slow and use a push pad. Slow travel across the blade will yield a fine cut.

Continue making passes on all four edges of the door center panel until the edge is slightly smaller than $^1/_4$". Use a heavy-duty blade and make small, slow passes with the door panel. Slower passes will also give you a finer cut, and a great deal of final sanding will be eliminated. The amount you raise the blade for each pass, as well as the travel across the blade, will depend on the wood used. Hardwood will be a lot more difficult than softwood, so make a few trial passes to gauge your speed and cut depth.

3 Sand the panel to remove all saw marks. Test fit the panel in the stiles and rails until you achieve a snug, but not tight, fit. Assemble the door using glue on the tenons only. Do not glue the panel, as it must float freely to account for expansion and contraction during humidity-level changes.

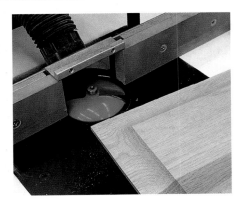

4 Raised-panel doors use solid-wood panels that have their edges milled. The panel face can be higher or on the same plane as the frame face. You can control the panel position by deciding upon the frame and panel thickness before starting to build a door.

To make a door with the raised-panel top surface on the same level as the frame members, use ³/₄"-thick frame boards with a ⁹/₁₆"-thick panel that fits in a groove, which is cut ³/₁₆" in from the back face of the frame members. Or you can use a combination of ⁷/₈"-thick frame pieces with a ⁵/₈" panel set ¹/₄" in from the back face of the frame members.

If you want the panel face raised above the frame member front faces, use the same material thickness for the frame and panel pieces. It's a style choice that you can decide upon after making a few sample doors.

Panels for these raised-panel doors are normally made by edge-gluing a number of solid boards. They can be attached with glue or with a combination of biscuits and glue. Both methods are commonly used, but biscuit joinery is becoming more popular.

In some cases, the panel can be one wide

board, but be careful with this situation, as a solid board tends to cup and warp more than a number of glued-up boards. Twisting door panels can quickly throw everything out of alignment. So, where possible, use a number of boards with growth pattern rings opposing each other to make your panels.

Remember a few words of caution before using the router panel-raising bits: They can remove a great deal of material in one pass, but that is dangerous and will not produce good results. Take many small passes, use high-quality bits with a ¹/₂" shaft, and take your time.

I use a panel-raising bit in a router table set up with a 2-hp router. The final height, or cut, with these bits should be set to leave a ¹/₄"-thick edge on the panel so it will fit snugly into the frame grooves. Again, make a number of small passes with these bits until the desired edge thickness is achieved.

Installing the Hidden Hinge

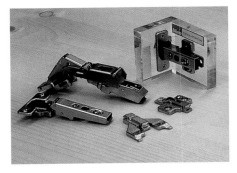

HIDDEN HINGES

The 100° to 120° European full-overlay hinge with a standard mounting plate is used in this system. The two exceptions are the 36" standard corner base cabinet, which uses two 170° full-overlay hinges and two bifold door hinges, and the 24" standard upper corner cabinet, which uses the 170° full-overlay door hinge with a face-frame mounting plate.

This building system uses the standard mounting plate that is attached to the side or carcass board. The upper corner cabinet side, because of its design, does not line up flush with the inside of the face-frame opening. For this reason we use a mounting plate that is designed to be attached to the cabinet face frame.

1 Drill 35mm, flat-bottom holes in the doors with a drill bit specifically designed for hinge installation, called a hinge-boring bit. I normally place the hole ¹/₈" in from the door edge, which properly orients the door on the cabinet. There isn't an absolutely correct position for these hinges, but I found installing them at 3" centers from the top and bottom of the door works well. Prior to drilling the hinge holes, note the position and side clearances required for pullouts or other accessories, particularly in the base cabinets.

Invest in the best carbide 35mm hinge drill that you can afford. The drill must provide a clean, accurate cut with minimal tear-out of wood fibers around the edge of the hole.

Use a face-frame mounting plate, shown attached to the hinge in the illustration, or the standard mounting plate. Attach the hinge body to the door with two ⁵/₈"-long screws.

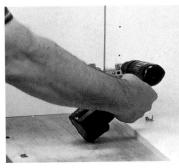

2 Mount the hinges and the hinge plates on the door in their 35mm holes. To get the door-to-cabinet spacing I place a ¹/₈" strip of wood between the door and the cabinet face frame.

I hold the door in place and put two screws in each hinge plate into the cabinet side. Then I remove the door and hinges from the hinge plates and finish screwing the plates to the cabinet side.

The only exceptions to this method are the wide-opening 170° hinges. In that instance I use a 100° to 120° hinge to mount the doors and locate the hinge plates. When the plates are mounted I replace the normal hinges with the 170s, as the plate position is identical for both.

Installing the doors flush with the bottom of the face frame on both upper and lower cabinets is important. This position gives us a 1¹/₄" face-frame reveal above the doors. This reveal allows for countertop-to-door clearance on the base units and a space to install decorative trim moulding above the doors on the upper cabinets.

A door, over the life of the kitchen, may be opened thousands of times, and therefore quality is an issue. I suggest you thoroughly investigate the hardware supplied in your area and choose the best product available.

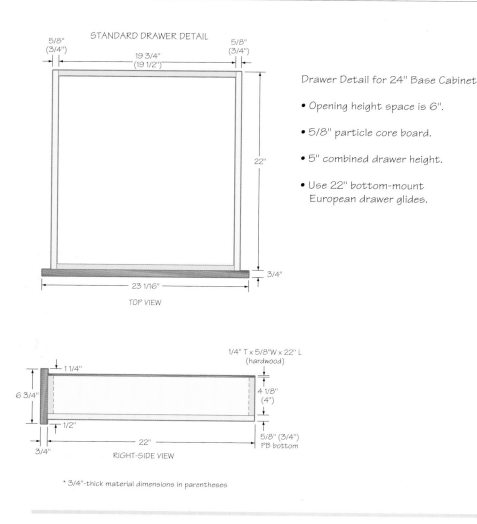

STANDARD DRAWER DETAIL

5/8"
(3/4")

19 3/4"
(19 1/2")

5/8"
(3/4")

22"

3/4"

23 1/16"

TOP VIEW

1 1/4"

6 3/4"

1/2"

3/4"

22"

RIGHT-SIDE VIEW

1/4" T x 5/8"W x 22" L
(hardwood)

4 1/8"
(4")

5/8" (3/4")
PB bottom

* 3/4"-thick material dimensions in parentheses

Drawer Detail for 24" Base Cabinet

- Opening height space is 6".
- 5/8" particle core board.
- 5" combined drawer height.
- Use 22" bottom-mount European drawer glides.

DRAWERS, PULLOUTS AND FLIP-OUTS

A high-quality drawer is a requirement. It should be solid, well constructed and easy to maintain. Drawers are subjected to a good deal of abuse by normal opening and closing. Spills can occur, grease and grime can build up on the interior, and wear on the movable parts is a fact of life.

The hardware I use is the simple and effective European-style bottom-mount drawer glide. It has been in use for many years and, according to many in the industry, is virtually trouble free. As an added bonus, the drawer hardware is easy to install.

I also use the strips of melamine-coated PB that are left over from the cutting of cabinet parts. These strips, sometimes as much as 7" wide, are ideal for the sides, backs and fronts of the drawer carcasses.

CALCULATING DRAWER SIZES

In general, the 1" rule applies to most drawer-building projects when using modern hardware. Bottom-mounted and side-mounted glides made by manufacturers such as Blum and Accuride require a $\frac{1}{2}$" space between the outside of the drawer box and the cabinet side for proper installation and operation.

The drawer opening is measured from inside the face frame, or cabinet sides if it's a frameless-style cabinet. Subtracting 1" from that dimension will give you the drawer box's outside width. To simplify matters, I also subtract 1" from the drawer opening height to determine my drawer box height.

This is a general rule and I suggest you read the manufacturer's instruc-

tions packed with your hardware. One important issue should be kept in mind if you plan to use the new hardware. Most drawer-glide systems are designed to operate based on frameless cabinet building styles. The cabinet side is the cabinet face, and therefore the opening equals the side's inside face-to-face dimension. But that doesn't mean the hardware cannot be used with face-frame-style cabinets.

If the face-frame inside width is smaller than the cabinet's inside width, cleats or spacers must be installed to mount the glides flush with the inside of the face frame. It's a simple matter of attaching small strips of wood to mount the hardware.

DRAWER-GLIDE HARDWARE

Bottom-mounted drawer glides, and most drawer glides, for that matter, are sold in 2" length increments. They start at 10" long and increase by 2" up to 36" in length.

If the inside dimension of your cabinet carcass is 22⅝", a 22"-long glide set must be used, because the next size at 24" long will not fit. Design your carcass depths keeping the glide-length sizing in mind.

Building the Drawer Box

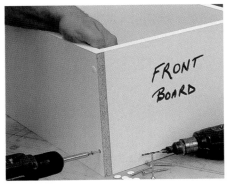

1 | Cut the drawer parts accurately, as there is little room for error. Drawer boxes can bind or fall out if the dimensions aren't correct, so this is one area of kitchen cabinetmaking that demands attention to detail.

Join the two sides to the back and front boards using 2" PB screws. Remember to always drill a pilot hole in the melamine PB to ensure maximum hold with screwed butt joinery. Space the screws about 8" apart.

The drawing illustrates a 21"-wide drawer box designed to be installed in a 24"-wide face-frame base cabinet. The stiles on this cabinet are 1" wide, therefore the inside dimension of the cabinet carcass is 22". The box is 1" less with respect to cabinet interior width.

There are slight differences in the dimensions between ⅝"- and ¾"-thick material, but all the same joinery principles apply to both.

2 | Cut the bottom board, making sure its dimensions are correct, and apply an iron-on edge tape to the two side edges. If this bottom board is cut square, it will square the drawer box.

Space 2"-long PB screws about 6" apart. Start at one corner, bring the edges flush and drive a screw into that corner to secure the joint. Proceed to the next corner, secure it and continue on to join the final two corners. Fill in the field with screws.

3 | Attach the drawer-glide box runners to the drawer carcass following the manufacturer's instructions. Normally the glides are installed with ⅝"-long screws and mounted flush to the front edge of the drawer box.

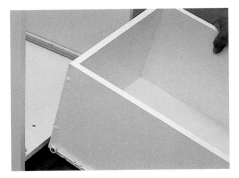

4 | Install the carcass runners with ⅝"-long screws. Use a framing square to draw a screw-hole guideline on the cabinet side. It must be located 90° to the cabinet's front edge for proper drawer operation.

5 | The drawer face is secured to the drawer box with 1"-long screws, driven through the back side of the front board into the face.

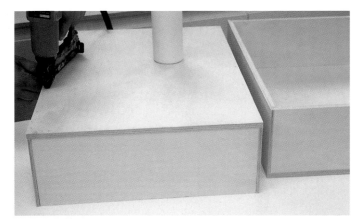

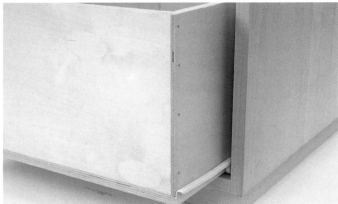

DRAWER BOX MATERIAL OPTIONS

Drawers can be fancy solid-wood styles with dovetails or simple melamine particleboard butt-joined boxes. In today's kitchen, drawer boxes are made to take abuse and be easily cleaned, so melamine PB is an obvious choice.

You may want to use plywood for a desk drawer in the kitchen, and cabinet-grade Baltic birch is a good choice. I often use $1/2$"-thick material and join the box, following the same procedures as butt-joined PB, using glue and brad nails.

To increase the joint strength when building drawer boxes using $1/2$"-thick Baltic birch, I cut $1/2$"-wide by $1/4$"-deep rabbets in the back and front boards. Applying glue to the joints and securing with brad nails creates a strong, solid drawer box.

BUILDING PULLOUTS

Pullouts in base and pantry cabinets have become extremely popular over the past few years. They are an effective storage option, and increase the ease of access when compared to standard shelves in a base cabinet.

I've constructed many styles of pullouts over the years. Some styles are directly dependent on client requirements. If a deep pullout is required, I use the drawer style as described previously. It can be as deep or shallow as the client requires. Deep pullouts may

be required for storing pots, dry goods or plastic containers.

In the last couple of years I have constructed the majority of pullouts using a $5/8$" sheet of melamine-coated PB, mounted on European drawer glides. The front exposed edge of the PB is covered with plastic cap moulding, and the remaining exposed edges of the PB have iron-on edge tape applied. A rail system, as shown in this photograph, can be installed on the PB pullout. This is a very effective system for pullout construction, and one that I recommend as the standard design. This surround rail is a commercial product and is often available through stores that carry a full line of kitchen cabinet hardware.

PULLOUTS BEHIND DOORS

Keep one important design consideration in mind when constructing and installing pullouts in a cabinet behind doors. The European hinge used in this design has the ability to open in less than the space it requires for door overlap. In effect, the door mounted with these hinges opens in a space less than $5/8$", which puts the edge of the door slightly inside the face-frame opening.

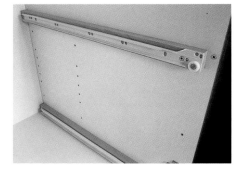

While this feature is beneficial, particularly when two doors are close together, it means that a pullout will rub or hit the door. To prevent this, install $3/4$"-thick by $1\frac{1}{2}$"-high cleats on the interior of the carcass, and mount the drawer glides to the cleats. The space occupied by these cleats must be taken into consideration when determining your pullout width.

If you cannot afford to reduce the width of your pullouts by using the cleat method, you can use 170°-opening hinges that clear the interior width of the face frame when fully opened. However, the cabinet door must be opened past the 90° position to clear the interior space. I tend to use the cleat method with the less-expensive 100° to 120° hinges in almost all situations.

BASE FACE-FRAME CABINET DETAIL (30" Base Shown)

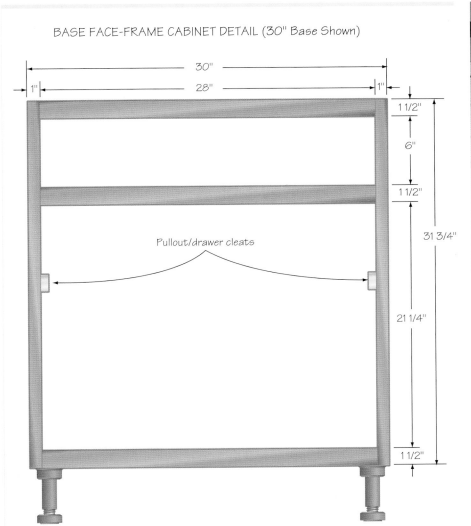

30"

28"

1" 1"

1 1/2"

6"

1 1/2"

31 3/4"

Pullout/drawer cleats

21 1/4"

1 1/2"

Pullouts are mounted on standard drawer-glide sets. They can be made with any sheet material or hardwood. Use a sheet veneer and hardwood sides to make great base pullout shelves. Or use white melamine PB sheets and 3"-high sides of the same material with edge tape applied to the exposed edges. Simply follow the drawer box construction procedures.

BUILDING FLIP-OUTS

Sink cabinets, normally a 36" standard base, are not usually fitted with $30\frac{1}{2}$" full cabinet-height doors. They are built as a drawer-over-door cabinet, so the underside of the sink is not visible when the cabinet doors are open. Because the sink occupies the space needed for the drawer carcass, the drawer has a false face and is nonoperational. Normally this space is lost, but various suppliers, such as Rev-A-Shelf, sell a flip-out kit that comes with hinges and a plastic tray. You can install this kit on the false drawer front and have a functional flip-out drawer face with a plastic tray inside that can be used to store scrubbing pads and dish soap. It's a popular option and an easy item to install. Your local kitchen hardware supply outlet should stock these kits.

BUILDING FRAMELESS CABINETS

FRAMELESS CONSTRUCTION PRINCIPLES

The European frameless cabinet is modular and commonly ranges in widths from 10" to 36". The frameless system offers flexibility with quality, and can be built with any $^{5}/_{8}$"- or $^{3}/_{4}$"-thick sheet material; we are not restricted to white cabinets.

The Europeans perfected the box, or unitized, construction methods to a point where the frameless cabinet, often called the Euro-style kitchen, has become a popular option in North America. European design features such as the hidden hinge, bottom-mount drawer glides and adjustable cabinet legs are now an important part of the North American cabinetmaking industry.

The frameless cabinet parts can be cut, drilled, edge banded, finished and all hardware installed before the box is assembled. If necessary, the cabinet boxes can be shipped unassembled to the work site, then assembled and installed on site. This type of construction is very easy and fast with top-of-the-line results.

The kitchen cabinet building system described in this chapter is based on that box-style construction. The techniques apply to cabinet carcasses and drawer assemblies. Think of the construction system in its basic form and don't get confused with thinking in terms of the finished product. If you break the system down to the box concept — four sides and a bottom — you'll quickly understand and appreciate the simplicity of the construction methods.

JOINERY

Butt joinery using particleboard screws is commonly used to build frameless cabinets.

The joints are almost all butt joints, secured with 2" screws designed specifically for particleboard material. The strength of the butt joint is due in large part to the holding ability of these screws. They are installed in a pre-drilled pilot hole and, because of their design, thread the hole, providing an extremely strong joint. When a panel is exposed, such as an end-of-run cabinet, biscuit joinery and glue is a preferred method because it's completely hidden.

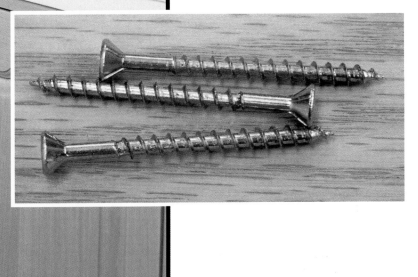

EDGE BANDING

Frameless cabinets do not have a face frame, so the edges are covered with tape. Many edge tape materials are available that will match any sheet material you wish to use. Melamine and veneer tapes, with heat-sensitive glue, are a common item in most woodworking stores.

Edge tapes are applied with an iron or, if you plan on doing a lot of frameless cabinet work, a hot-air edge-banding station. The tape is applied to all visible edges on frameless cabinets.

MATERIALS

You have many sheet material options for building frameless cabinets. You can use particleboard, plywood or medium-density fiberboards. Particleboards are coated with paper and epoxy resin to create melamine particleboards in dozens of colors and textures. Wood-veneers are put on particleboard, plywood and medium density fiberboard. Many have an edge tape to match the surface material.

I suggest you use $^5/_8$"- or $^3/_4$"-thick melamine particleboard material as your standard for carcass construction. As discussed, it's strong and able to accommodate the loading capacity that kitchen cabinets are often required to handle. A full $^5/_8$"- or $^3/_4$"-thick back should also be standard. It provides many advantages, including the elimination of cabinet mounting strips that are normally seen on the inside top and bottom of cabinets. You'll end up with a stronger cabinet that stays square, reducing the twisting and racking that sometimes occurs during installation.

A commercial sheet material may be available in your area, that has a wood veneer on one side and a melamine coating on the opposite face. It's a great product to use when building frameless cabinets because you get the tough

melamine finish on the inside with a wood-veneer exterior. This sheet material is commonly used by frameless cabinetmakers, and you'll often see examples in your local home or kitchen cabinet store.

As discussed in chapters three and four, make certain all boards are cut square and properly dimensioned. The two most critical boards, in terms of dimension, are the top and bottom, as they determine the inside width of the cabinet.

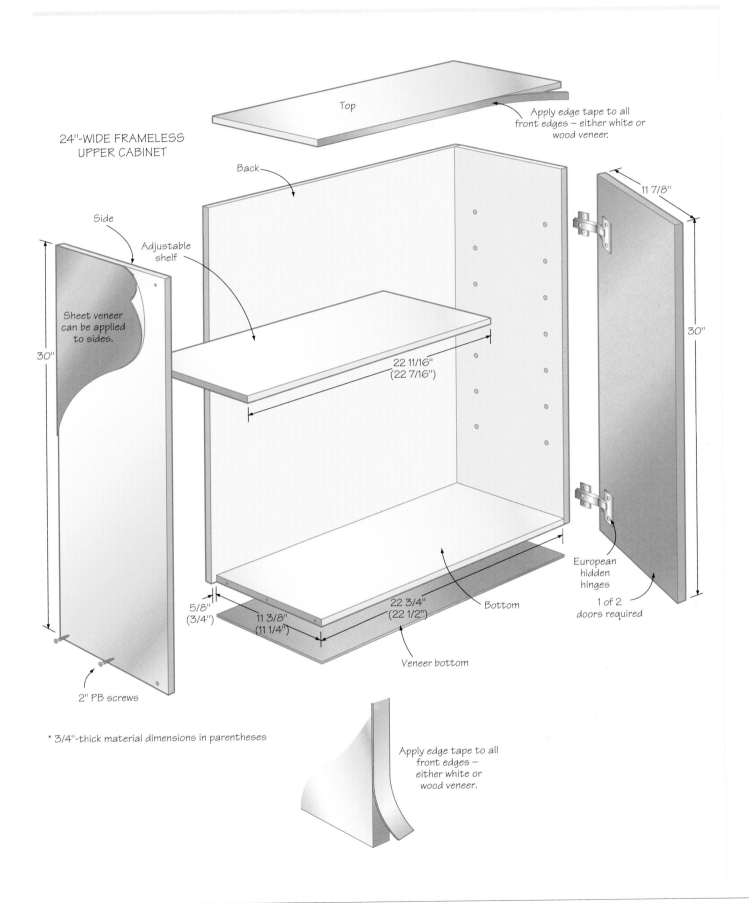

24"-WIDE FRAMELESS
UPPER CABINET

Top

Apply edge tape to all
front edges – either white or
wood veneer.

Back

11 7/8"

Side

Adjustable
shelf

Sheet veneer
can be applied
to sides.

30"

30"

22 11/16"
(22 7/16")

European
hidden
hinges

1 of 2
doors required

5/8"
(3/4")

11 3/8"
(11 1/4")

22 3/4"
(22 1/2")

Bottom

Veneer bottom

2" PB screws

* 3/4"-thick material dimensions in parentheses

Apply edge tape to all
front edges –
either white or
wood veneer.

Building Upper Frameless Cabinets

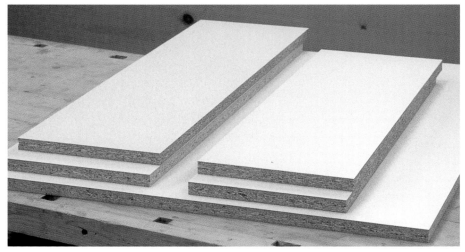

CALCULATING CABINET SIZE

I've created a cutting list for $^5/_8$"- and $^3/_4$"-thick sheet material, for many of the common frameless cabinet widths. However, you can calculate any width; you are not restricted to standard-size cabinets.

For example, a plan calls for an upper cabinet that's $27^1/_2$" wide by 30" high by 12" deep with two shelves and two doors. That's all the information needed to create a cutting list. In this example I'll use $^3/_4$"-thick melamine particleboard to build the cabinet.

Cabinet width is always the front dimension. A $27^1/_2$"-wide upper cabinet requires a bottom and top board that are $11^1/_4$" deep by 26" wide. The $11^1/_4$" depth plus the $^3/_4$"-thick back gives us a standard 12"-deep upper cabinet carcass. The 26"-wide top and bottom board, plus the thickness of two sides, equals our required cabinet width.

Side boards, or gables, are the same depth as the top and bottom boards at $11^1/_4$", and the full height of the finished cabinet at 30". The backboard equals the width and height of the finished cabinet, or $27^1/_2$" (plus $^1/_8$") wide by 30" high. Notice, as we did with the face-frame style of cabinets, the backboard is cut $^1/_8$" wider to allow for any material thickness variances. The back can be trimmed to size just before it's installed. The adjustable shelves are the same depth as the top and bottom boards, and are normally $^1/_{16}$" shorter in width

1 Cut the $^5/_8$"- or $^3/_4$"-thick carcass parts to size. Use a table saw to cut the sides, bottom and top, back and two shelf boards to the proper dimensions. A table saw with a melamine particleboard blade will cut all the pieces cleanly. Number the parts as detailed on your cutting list and illustrations, following the procedures described in chapter twelve.

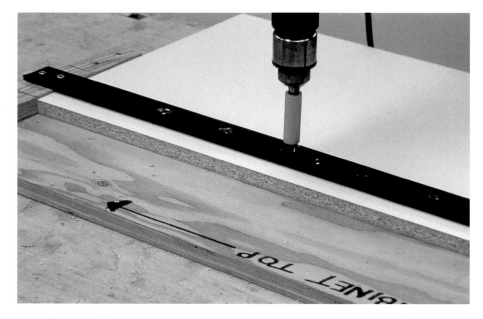

2 Drill the holes in each side board for the adjustable shelves, if needed. Be sure to mark the top of each panel. I normally start and end my columns of holes about 4" from the top and bottom edges. The hole columns are placed 1" in from the back and front edges and are the diameter required for the shelf pins you plan to use.

to permit easy movement in the cabinet.

Door width is found using the same 1"-plus formula as previously detailed. The inside cabinet dimension of 26" plus 1" equals one door width. We need two doors, so dividing 27" by 2 means each door must be $13^1/_2$" wide. Door height on frameless upper cabinets usually equals cabinet height, or 30".

CUTTING LIST FOR UPPER CABINETS USING $^5/_8$" (16MM) THICK SHEET MATERIAL – INCHES (MILLIMETERS)

CABINET WIDTH	CABINET BOX TWO SIDES DEPTH × HEIGHT		TOP & BOTTOM DEPTH × WIDTH		BACK WIDTH × HEIGHT		SHELF SIZE		DOOR WIDTH × 30" HIGH (762)	
12 (305)	$11^3/_8 \times 30$	(289 × 762)	$11^3/_8 \times 10^3/_4$	(289 × 273)	$12^1/_8 \times 30$	(308 × 762)	$11^3/_8 \times 10^{11}/_{16}$	(289 × 272)	1 @ $11^3/_4$	(298)
15 (381)	$11^3/_8 \times 30$	(289 × 762)	$11^3/_8 \times 13^3/_4$	(289 × 349)	$15^1/_8 \times 30$	(384 × 762)	$11^3/_8 \times 13^{11}/_{16}$	(289 × 348)	1 @ $14^3/_4$	(375)
18 (457)	$11^3/_8 \times 30$	(289 × 762)	$11^3/_8 \times 16^3/_4$	(289 × 425)	$18^1/_8 \times 30$	(460 × 762)	$11^3/_8 \times 16^{11}/_{16}$	(289 × 424)	1 @ $17^3/_4$	(451)
21 (533)	$11^3/_8 \times 30$	(289 × 762)	$11^3/_8 \times 19^3/_4$	(289 × 502)	$21^1/_8 \times 30$	(536 × 762)	$11^3/_8 \times 19^{11}/_{16}$	(289 × 501)	2 @ $10^3/_8$	(264)
24 (610)	$11^3/_8 \times 30$	(289 × 762)	$11^3/_8 \times 22^3/_4$	(289 × 578)	$24^1/_8 \times 30$	(613 × 762)	$11^3/_8 \times 22^{11}/_{16}$	(289 × 577)	2 @ $11^7/_8$	(301)
27 (686)	$11^3/_8 \times 30$	(289 × 762)	$11^3/_8 \times 25^3/_4$	(289 × 654)	$27^1/_8 \times 30$	(689 × 762)	$11^3/_8 \times 25^{11}/_{16}$	(289 × 653)	2 @ $13^3/_8$	(340)
30 (762)	$11^3/_8 \times 30$	(289 × 762)	$11^3/_8 \times 28^3/_4$	(289 × 730)	$30^1/_8 \times 30$	(765 × 762)	$11^3/_8 \times 28^{11}/_{16}$	(289 × 729)	2 @ $14^7/_8$	(378)
33 (838)	$11^3/_8 \times 30$	(289 × 762)	$11^3/_8 \times 31^3/_4$	(289 × 806)	$33^1/_8 \times 30$	(841 × 762)	$11^3/_8 \times 31^{11}/_{16}$	(289 × 805)	2 @ $16^3/_8$	(416)
36 (914)	$11^3/_8 \times 30$	(289 × 762)	$11^3/_8 \times 34^3/_4$	(289 × 883)	$36^1/_8 \times 30$	(917 × 762)	$11^3/_8 \times 34^{11}/_{16}$	(289 × 882)	2 @ $17^7/_8$	(454)

CUTTING LIST FOR UPPER CABINETS USING $^3/_4$" (19MM) THICK SHEET MATERIAL – INCHES (MILLIMETERS)

CABINET WIDTH	CABINET BOX TWO SIDES DEPTH × HEIGHT		TOP & BOTTOM DEPTH × WIDTH		BACK WIDTH × HEIGHT		SHELF SIZE		DOOR WIDTH × 30" HIGH (762)	
12 (305)	$11^1/_4 \times 30$	(285 × 762)	$11^1/_4 \times 10^1/_2$	(285 × 267)	$12^1/_8 \times 30$	(308 × 762)	$11^1/_4 \times 10^7/_{16}$	(285 × 265)	1 @ $11^1/_2$	(292)
15 (381)	$11^1/_4 \times 30$	(285 × 762)	$11^1/_4 \times 13^1/_2$	(285 × 343)	$15^1/_8 \times 30$	(384 × 762)	$11^1/_4 \times 13^7/_{16}$	(285 × 341)	1 @ $14^1/_2$	(369)
18 (457)	$11^1/_4 \times 30$	(285 × 762)	$11^1/_4 \times 16^1/_2$	(285 × 419)	$18^1/_8 \times 30$	(460 × 762)	$11^1/_4 \times 16^7/_{16}$	(285 × 417)	1 @ $17^1/_2$	(445)
21 (533)	$11^1/_4 \times 30$	(285 × 762)	$11^1/_4 \times 19^1/_2$	(285 × 496)	$21^1/_8 \times 30$	(536 × 762)	$11^1/_4 \times 19^7/_{16}$	(285 × 494)	2 @ $10^1/_4$	(260)
24 (610)	$11^1/_4 \times 30$	(285 × 762)	$11^1/_4 \times 22^1/_2$	(285 × 572)	$24^1/_8 \times 30$	(613 × 762)	$11^1/_4 \times 22^7/_{16}$	(285 × 570)	2 @ $11^3/_4$	(298)
27 (686)	$11^1/_4 \times 30$	(285 × 762)	$11^1/_4 \times 25^1/_2$	(285 × 648)	$27^1/_8 \times 30$	(689 × 762)	$11^1/_4 \times 25^7/_{16}$	(285 × 646)	2 @ $13^1/_4$	(336)
30 (762)	$11^1/_4 \times 30$	(285 × 762)	$11^1/_4 \times 28^1/_2$	(285 × 724)	$30^1/_8 \times 30$	(765 × 762)	$11^1/_4 \times 28^7/_{16}$	(285 × 722)	2 @ $14^3/_4$	(375)
33 (838)	$11^1/_4 \times 30$	(285 × 762)	$11^1/_4 \times 31^1/_2$	(285 × 800)	$33^1/_8 \times 30$	(841 × 762)	$11^1/_4 \times 31^7/_{16}$	(285 × 798)	2 @ $16^1/_4$	(412)
36 (914)	$11^1/_4 \times 30$	(285 × 762)	$11^1/_4 \times 34^1/_2$	(285 × 877)	$36^1/_8 \times 30$	(917 × 762)	$11^1/_4 \times 34^7/_{16}$	(285 × 875)	2 @ $17^3/_4$	(451)

3 Apply edge tape to all edges that will be visible once the cabinet is built. Normally the front and bottom edges of the side boards, the front edges of the top and bottom boards, the side and bottom edges of the backboard, and the front edges of the shelves are taped.

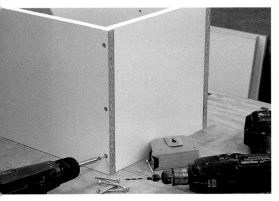

4 Fasten one side board to the edge of the bottom board, making sure the joint is square and flush. Drill a $\frac{1}{8}$" countersunk pilot hole for each of the three 2" PB screws. Do not overtighten. Take care as well to drill the pilot hole so that it's in the center of the edge on the board you are fastening the side to; in this case, the bottom board of the carcass. Connect the remaining three corner butt joints in the same manner.

You can use biscuits, dowels or confirmat screws. With this frameless style of cabinetry, end gables that are exposed on any side will generally have a cover panel or, if left exposed, will be joined with biscuits.

5 For purposes of verification at this point, referencing a 24"-wide upper cabinet as an example, you should have a four-sided box with inside dimensions of $22\frac{3}{4}$" (the width of the bottom and top carcass boards) by $28\frac{3}{4}$" high (the length of the side minus the thickness of the top and bottom carcass boards when using $\frac{5}{8}$" sheet material).

Measure the actual width of the carcass. If the sheet material is slightly thicker than $\frac{5}{8}$" or $\frac{3}{4}$", your carcass will be wider than planned. The backboard was cut slightly wider to accommodate that possibility. Trim the back to the correct size before attaching it to the carcass.

Secure the backboard to the carcass, flush with all edges of the box. This will force the cabinet corners into square. Install 2" PB screws at 6" centers around the perimeter of the back. Secure the first corner, aligning it square, then secure the remaining three corners while aligning the box. Finally, install screws between the corners. Always drill a pilot hole for the screws, as this will guarantee the best hold possible. Use a marking gauge to draw lines $\frac{5}{16}$" (or $\frac{3}{8}$" for $\frac{3}{4}$"-thick board) in from the edges as a guide for the pilot holes.

6 Choose the style of door you would like to install. Door height for upper frameless cabinets with this building system is 30" high. The width of each door is dependent on the size of the carcass. Use the 1" rule as discussed in previous chapters. To review, the doors are 1" wider than the inside side-to-side distance. If you require two doors, simply divide the door width by two.

Drill a 35mm-diameter hole, 3" on center, from each end of the door, $\frac{1}{8}$" away from the door's edge. Use a hinge-boring bit to drill the hole $\frac{1}{2}$" deep, or as specified by the hinge supplier.

Attach a 100° to 120° standard-opening hinge with two $\frac{5}{8}$" screws, using a square to make sure the hinge arm is at 90° to the door's edge. This is important because the hinge must be properly mounted to function correctly. Once the hinges are secure, attach the hinge plate to each hinge.

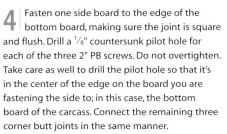

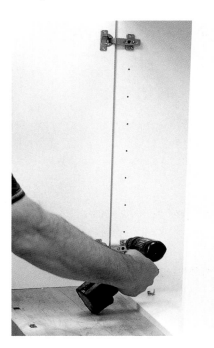

7 Hold the door in its normally open position, with the hinge and plate attached to the door, and place a $\frac{1}{8}$"-thick spacer between the cabinet's front edge and the back edge of the door. Drive screws through the hinge plate and into the cabinet side to secure the doors.

8 To complete the standard upper cabinet, install shelf pins, test fit the shelves and attach handles or knobs of your choice. The shelf's front edge can be covered with iron-on melamine edge tape, a plastic cap moulding that's available at your local home store or wood edge trim to match the doors.

BUILDING A 24" FRAMELESS UPPER CORNER CABINET

This special upper corner cabinet is not as straightforward as the standard upper cabinets, and does require a little extra attention during construction. The building style that's illustrated is one of the two or three construction methods that can be used. This is the construction style I use and, I believe, is one of the better methods of building an upper corner cabinet.

This cabinet is called a 24" upper corner because it covers 24" on each wall of a corner. The face is at a 45° angle to the cabinets on either side. Dead space, often found in corner wall cabinets, is minimized by the installation of a two-shelf lazy Susan assembly.

As illustrated in the tables, pay particular attention to the backboard cut sizes. One back is ⁵⁄₈" or ³⁄₄" wider to allow for the required overlaps of the boards during assembly.

CUTTING LIST FOR A 24" (610MM) UPPER CORNER CABINET USING ⁵⁄₈" (16MM) THICK SHEET MATERIAL

inches (millimeters)

REFERENCE	QUANTITY	PART	STOCK	THICKNESS	(mm)	WIDTH	(mm)	LENGTH	(mm)	COMMENTS
A	2	sides	melamine pb	⁵⁄₈	(16)	11³⁄₈	(289)	30	(762)	
B	2	top & bottom	melamine pb	⁵⁄₈	(16)	22³⁄₄	(578)	22³⁄₄	(578)	cut as illustrated
C	1	back	melamine pb	⁵⁄₈	(16)	23³⁄₈	(594)	30	(762)	
D	1	back	melamine pb	⁵⁄₈	(16)	24	(610)	30	(762)	
E	1	door	melamine pb	⁵⁄₈	(16)	15³⁄₄	(400)	30-high	(762)	
F	2	stiles	melamine pb	⁵⁄₈	(16)	2	(51)	28³⁄₄-high	(730)	install as detailed with 45° corner blocks

CUTTING LIST FOR A 24" (610MM) UPPER CORNER CABINET USING ³⁄₄" (19MM) THICK SHEET MATERIAL

inches (millimeters)

REFERENCE	QUANTITY	PART	STOCK	THICKNESS	(mm)	WIDTH	(mm)	LENGTH	(mm)	COMMENTS
A	2	sides	melamine pb	³⁄₄	(19)	11¹⁄₄	(285)	30	(762)	
B	2	top & bottom	melamine pb	³⁄₄	(19)	22¹⁄₂	(572)	22¹⁄₂	(572)	cut as illustrated
C	1	back	melamine pb	³⁄₄	(19)	23¹⁄₄	(590)	30	(762)	
D	1	back	melamine pb	³⁄₄	(19)	24	(610)	30	(762)	
E	1	door	melamine pb	³⁄₄	(19)	15¹⁄₂	(394)	30-high	(762)	
F	2	stiles	melamine pb	³⁄₄	(19)	2	(51)	28¹⁄₂-high	(724)	install as detailed with 45° corner blocks

24" FRAMELESS UPPER CORNER CABINET

- An 18"-diameter lazy Susan is suggested.

- Door is 15 3/4" wide by 30" high with 5/8" material.
  Door is 15 1/2" wide by 30" high with 3/4" material.

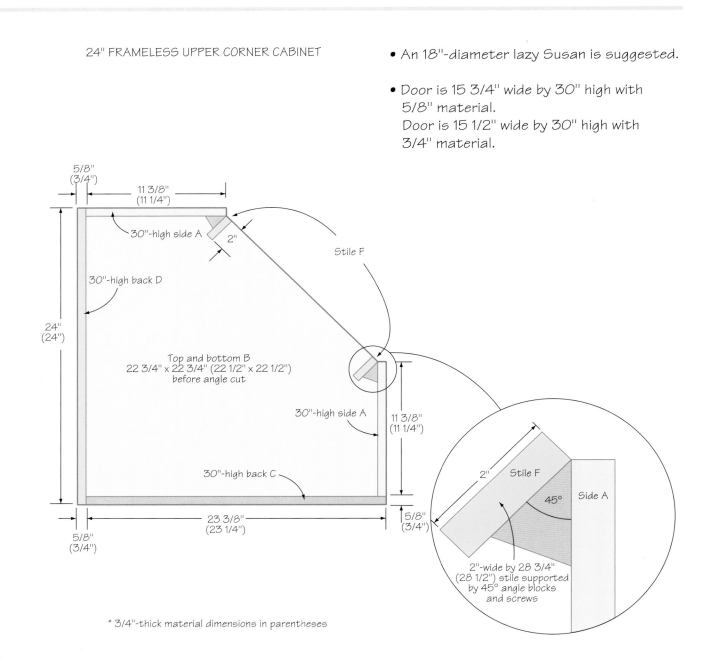

5/8"
(3/4")

11 3/8"
(11 1/4")

30"-high side A

2"

Stile F

30"-high back D

24"
(24")

Top and bottom B
22 3/4" x 22 3/4" (22 1/2" x 22 1/2")
before angle cut

30"-high side A

11 3/8"
(11 1/4")

30"-high back C

23 3/8"
(23 1/4")

5/8"
(3/4")

5/8"
(3/4")

2"

Stile F

45°

Side A

2"-wide by 28 3/4"
(28 1/2") stile supported
by 45° angle blocks
and screws

* 3/4"-thick material dimensions in parentheses

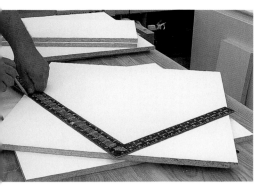

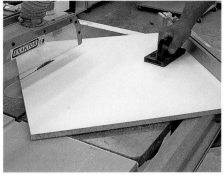

1 | Six boards are required for this cabinet; cut as indicated. This cabinet is almost always fitted with a two-shelf, 18"-diameter round lazy Susan assembly, and therefore holes for adjustable shelves are not required.

2 | Mark the angle cuts on the top and bottom boards. If you have a sliding table on your saw, or an angle-cutting jig, prepare the boards as indicated in the drawing. You can cut the front angles with a circular saw or jigsaw, keeping $1/8$" away from the line, then dress the boards to the line with a belt sander. Take your time and you'll get an accurate cut with minimum chipping of the melamine coating.

3 | Apply edge tape to all the boards that will have their edges exposed after the cabinet has been installed. If cabinets will be on either side, the side edges of the backs do not have to be covered. Don't forget to edge-tape the bottom edges of all panels.

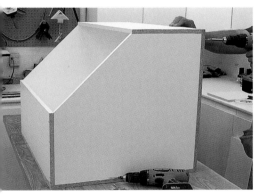

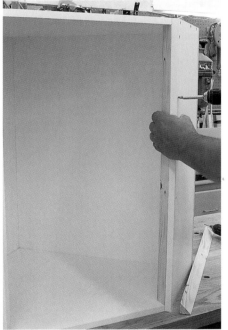

4 | Assemble the carcass as detailed in the technical drawing, with the exception of the two stiles and corner blocks. Use 2"-long particleboard screws in pilot holes to secure all the cabinet parts.

5 | Cut two wood strips $1^{3}/_{4}$" wide across the angled face, and equal to the length of the stiles (detailed in the cutting lists) with a 45° ripped edge running the length of each strip. Fasten the strips to the cabinet sides, about $1/16$" behind the front inside edge of each gable, using 1"-long screws through the outside face of each side panel.

6 | The two stiles are made using the same material as the cabinet carcass. Apply edge tape to both front and back long edges. Place each stile in the cabinet with one edge at 90° to the top and bottom boards' front edge. The stile corner should be held tight to the gable corner edge on each side and rest against the wood strips.

Drive $1^{1}/_{2}$"-long particleboard screws through the top and bottom boards into the ends of each stile. Install four additional screws on each side through the face of each stile into the wood strip. Both stiles should be securely held in place.

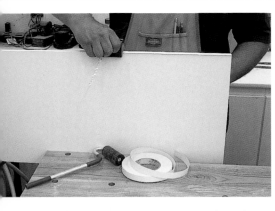

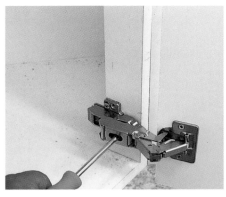

7 Cut the door to the size indicated based on the thickness of material you are using. Apply edge tape to all four edges of the door.

8 Drill hinge holes in the door and install standard hinges and plates as previously detailed. Hold the door in its normally open position with a $^1/_8$"-thick spacer between the door and cabinet stile edge. Attach the hinges to one 2"-wide stile and test the door operation.

9 Leave the hinge plates in place on the stiles. Remove the standard-opening hinges and replace them with 170°-opening hinges. The wide-swing hinges are necessary on this angled corner cabinet for easy access to the interior. Install a two-shelf, 18"-diameter, full-round lazy Susan, following the manufacturer's instructions, to complete the cabinet.

FRAMELESS BASE CABINETS

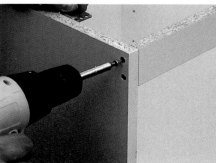

The basic frameless base cabinet is a box with two sides, called gable ends, a bottom board and a backboard. There is normally a door or door-and-drawer combination with fixed or adjustable shelving inside the cabinet.

All cabinets are not the same width. We often need specific width cabinets to fill dedicated spaces. If the width required doesn't match the sizes in the chart, follow the procedures described in "Calculating Cabinet Size" earlier in this chapter.

Standard base cabinets are 36" high when complete. That height accounts for the cabinet base support and the countertop thickness. For these cabinets I will be using plastic adjustable legs, but you can construct a wood base just as easily.

Frameless base cabinets do not need a top board, because the countertop covers the cabinet, but they do require an upper rail so the door clears the countertop. For my cabinets, I install a 2"-high rail as shown in this photograph. The height is constant regardless of the cabinet width, and the rail width is equal to the bottom board's width.

MATERIAL PROPERTIES

As discussed earlier in this chapter, the backboard is cut $^1/_8$" wider to allow for any material thickness variances. The back can be trimmed to size just before it's installed. The adjustable shelves are the same depth as the top and bottom boards, and normally $^1/_{16}$" shorter in width to permit easy movement in the cabinet.

BUILDING FRAMELESS BASE CABINETS

CUTTING LIST FOR BASE CABINETS USING $5/8$" (16MM) THICK SHEET MATERIAL – INCHES (MILLIMETERS)

CABINET WIDTH	CABINET BOX								SHELF SIZE		DOOR WIDTH × 30" HIGH (762)	
	TWO SIDES DEPTH × HEIGHT		TOP & BOTTOM DEPTH × WIDTH		BACK WIDTH × HEIGHT							
12 (305)	$23^3/8 \times 31$	(594 × 787)	$23^3/8 \times 10^3/4$	(594 × 273)	$12^1/8 \times 31$	(308 × 787)		$23^3/8 \times 10^{11}/16$	(594 × 272)	1 @ $11^3/4$	(298)
15 (381)	$23^3/8 \times 31$	(594 × 787)	$23^3/8 \times 13^3/4$	(594 × 349)	$15^1/8 \times 31$	(384 × 787)		$23^3/8 \times 13^{11}/16$	(594 × 348)	1 @ $14^3/4$	(375)
18 (457)	$23^3/8 \times 31$	(594 × 787)	$23^3/8 \times 16^3/4$	(594 × 425)	$18^1/8 \times 31$	(460 × 787)		$23^3/8 \times 16^{11}/16$	(594 × 424)	1 @ $17^3/4$	(451)
21 (533)	$23^3/8 \times 31$	(594 × 787)	$23^3/8 \times 19^3/4$	(594 × 502)	$21^1/8 \times 31$	(536 × 787)		$23^3/8 \times 19^{11}/16$	(594 × 501)	2 @ $10^3/8$	(264)
24 (610)	$23^3/8 \times 31$	(594 × 787)	$23^3/8 \times 22^3/4$	(594 × 578)	$24^1/8 \times 31$	(613 × 787)		$23^3/8 \times 22^{11}/16$	(594 × 577)	2 @ $11^7/8$	(301)
27 (686)	$23^3/8 \times 31$	(594 × 787)	$23^3/8 \times 25^3/4$	(594 × 654)	$27^1/8 \times 31$	(689 × 787)		$23^3/8 \times 25^{11}/16$	(594 × 653)	2 @ $13^3/8$	(340)
30 (762)	$23^3/8 \times 31$	(594 × 787)	$23^3/8 \times 28^3/4$	(594 × 730)	$30^1/8 \times 31$	(765 × 787)		$23^3/8 \times 28^{11}/16$	(594 × 729)	2 @ $14^7/8$	(378)
33 (838)	$23^3/8 \times 31$	(594 × 787)	$23^3/8 \times 31^3/4$	(594 × 806)	$33^1/8 \times 31$	(841 × 787)		$23^3/8 \times 31^{11}/16$	(594 × 805)	2 @ $16^3/8$	(416)
36 (914)	$23^3/8 \times 31$	(594 × 787)	$23^3/8 \times 34^3/4$	(594 × 883)	$36^1/8 \times 31$	(917 × 787)		$23^3/8 \times 34^{11}/16$	(594 × 882)	2 @ $17^7/8$	(454)

CUTTING LIST FOR BASE CABINETS USING $3/4$" (19MM) THICK SHEET MATERIAL – INCHES (MILLIMETERS)

CABINET WIDTH	CABINET BOX								SHELF SIZE		DOOR WIDTH × 30" HIGH (762)	
	TWO SIDES DEPTH × HEIGHT		TOP & BOTTOM DEPTH × WIDTH		BACK WIDTH × HEIGHT							
12 (305)	$23^1/4 \times 31$	(590 × 787)	$11^1/4 \times 10^1/2$	(285 × 267)	$12^1/8 \times 31$	(308 × 787)		$23^1/4 \times 10^7/16$	(590 × 265)	1 @ $11^1/2$	(292)
15 (381)	$23^1/4 \times 31$	(590 × 787)	$11^1/4 \times 13^1/2$	(285 × 343)	$15^1/8 \times 31$	(384 × 787)		$23^1/4 \times 13^7/16$	(590 × 341)	1 @ $14^1/2$	(369)
18 (457)	$23^1/4 \times 31$	(590 × 787)	$11^1/4 \times 16^1/2$	(285 × 419)	$18^1/8 \times 31$	(460 × 787)		$23^1/4 \times 16^7/16$	(590 × 417)	1 @ $17^1/2$	(445)
21 (533)	$23^1/4 \times 31$	(590 × 787)	$11^1/4 \times 19^1/2$	(285 × 496)	$21^1/8 \times 31$	(536 × 787)		$23^1/4 \times 19^7/16$	(590 × 494)	2 @ $10^1/4$	(260)
24 (610)	$23^1/4 \times 31$	(590 × 787)	$11^1/4 \times 22^1/2$	(285 × 572)	$24^1/8 \times 31$	(613 × 787)		$23^1/4 \times 22^7/16$	(590 × 570)	2 @ $11^3/4$	(298)
27 (686)	$23^1/4 \times 31$	(590 × 787)	$11^1/4 \times 25^1/2$	(285 × 648)	$27^1/8 \times 31$	(689 × 787)		$23^1/4 \times 25^7/16$	(590 × 646)	2 @ $13^1/4$	(336)
30 (762)	$23^1/4 \times 31$	(590 × 787)	$11^1/4 \times 28^1/2$	(285 × 724)	$30^1/8 \times 31$	(765 × 787)		$23^1/4 \times 28^7/16$	(590 × 722)	2 @ $14^3/4$	(375)
33 (838)	$23^1/4 \times 31$	(590 × 787)	$11^1/4 \times 31^1/2$	(285 × 800)	$33^1/8 \times 31$	(841 × 787)		$23^1/4 \times 31^7/16$	(590 × 798)	2 @ $16^1/4$	(412)
36 (914)	$23^1/4 \times 31$	(590 × 787)	$11^1/4 \times 34^1/2$	(285 × 877)	$36^1/8 \times 31$	(917 × 787)		$23^1/4 \times 34^7/16$	(590 × 875)	2 @ $17^3/4$	(451)

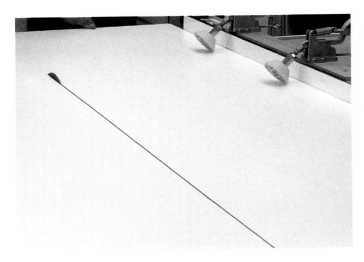

1 Cut all the parts as detailed in the cutting list charts, or based on your calculations for cabinet widths not detailed. Use a particleboard blade on your table saw and carefully cut the parts. The rails for each cabinet are the same width as the bottom board and 2" high. One rail is needed for each standard full-door base cabinet.

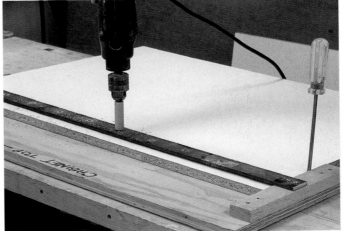

2 Drill holes for the adjustable shelf pins. These holes can be drilled using the homemade jig shown in chapter three. Shelf hole spacing is a matter of personal taste; however, I normally space them $1^1/4$" on center.

If you plan to install pullout shelves (see chapter nine) in the base cabinets, the holes for adjustable shelves aren't required and you can skip this step.

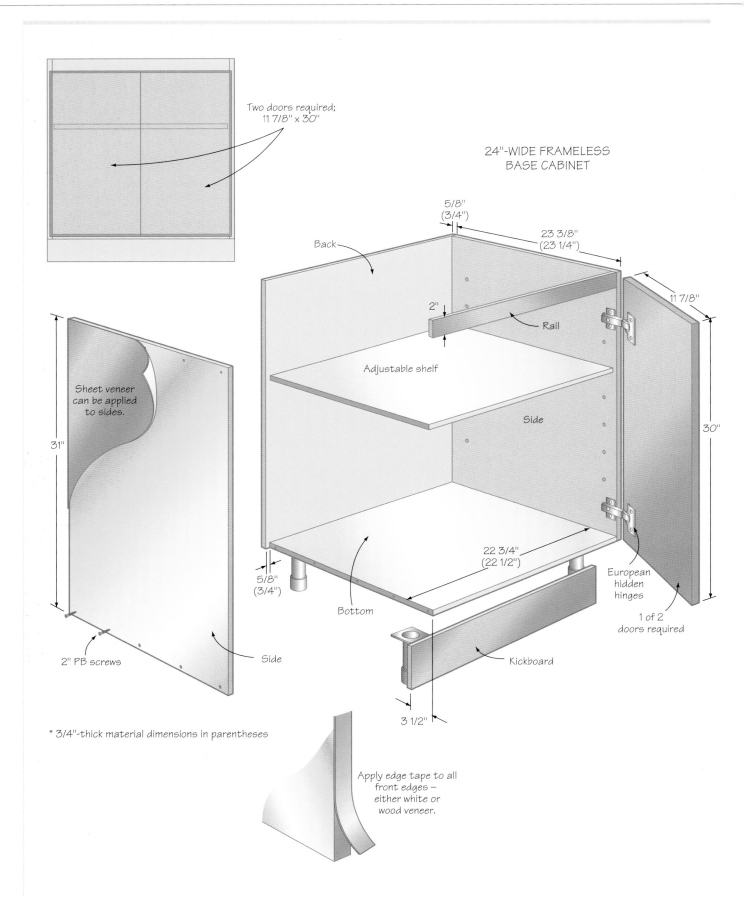

Two doors required;
11 7/8" x 30"

24"-WIDE FRAMELESS
BASE CABINET

5/8"
(3/4")

23 3/8"
(23 1/4")

Back

2"

11 7/8"

Rail

Adjustable shelf

Side

Sheet veneer
can be applied
to sides.

31"

30"

Side

22 3/4"
(22 1/2")

5/8"
(3/4")

European
hidden
hinges

Bottom

2" PB screws

Side

1 of 2
doors required

Kickboard

3 1/2"

* 3/4"-thick material dimensions in parentheses

Apply edge tape to all
front edges —
either white or
wood veneer.

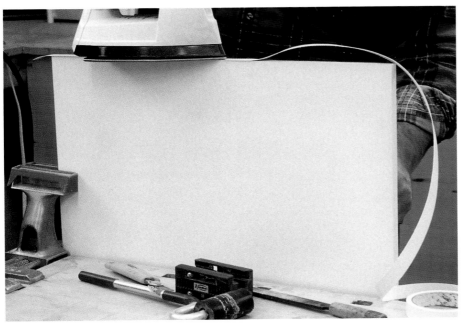

3 Apply edge tape to the exposed edges of the sides, bottom and underside of the top rail. The easiest tape to apply is heat activated. Trim the excess edge tape after ensuring it is firmly cemented to the board. Use an inexpensive hand trimmer to remove the excess tape on the sides. This task can be accomplished with a sharp file or knife. I've had the most success with a hand trimmer that costs about $20, found in most home stores.

4 Secure the sides to the bottom board as shown. Use 2" screws designed for particleboard joinery. The lower edges of the sides are aligned flush with the bottom face of the bottom board. Space the screws about 6" apart and always predrill and countersink the screw holes.

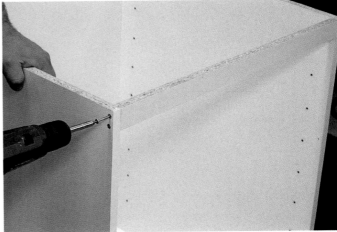

5 The back is attached with 2"-long PB screws about 6" apart. Measure the actual width of the bottom board, plus the two sides, then cut the backboard width to that measurement. Remember, the backboard was cut $^1/_8$" wider to account for any thickness differences in your material.

Ensure the backboard is flush with the top back edges of the side boards, the bottom edge of the base board and the outside edges of the side boards. This board will strengthen and square the cabinet.

6 Secure the 2"-high rail to the base cabinet, flush with the top edges of the side boards. Install one 2"-long screw per side in predrilled pilot holes.

These screws are close to the edges of the rail and it could split. The common practice, when joining particleboard material, is to keep screws at least 1" away from a board's edge. Drive one 2" screw at the center point of the rail and secure the back, on each side, with a right-angle countertop bracket. These brackets will be discussed later in this section.

7 | Attach four adjustable legs, one per corner, $3^1/_2$" back from the front edge. Secure them with $^5/_8$"-long PB screws so they support the side boards. At one time these legs were attached with a long bolt through the bottom board. However, many people use four $^5/_8$" screws because the legs can be easily moved, and cover caps are no longer needed to hide the bolt heads inside the cabinet.

8 | Install eight countertop brackets, two per inside face, on the sides, back and rail board. These are secured with $^5/_8$" PB screws and aligned flush with the cabinet's top edge.

9 | Edge-tape the doors with iron-on tape. Drill two 35mm holes in each door, $^1/_8$" back from the door edge and 3" on center from the bottom and top. These holes will be used to attach the hidden hinges.

11 | It's easy to guarantee perfect door placement using this simple installation method. First, cut a $^1/_8$"-thick spacer. Then place the door in its normally open position, making sure the vertical alignment is correct. Place the spacer strip between the door and cabinet side edge. Insert screws through the hinge plate and into the cabinet side board. After both hinges are secure, remove the door from the hinge plates and install the screws in the plate that are hidden by the hinge. Reinstall the doors and adjust if necessary.

Notice that I've placed a block under the cabinet. The cabinet bottom and door rest on this block so it will be held flush with the lower side of the bottom board while I attach the door.

10 | Screw the hinges in place with the hinge plates attached. I am using Blum 100° clip-on full-overlay hinges on my cabinet. The hinge is properly installed when it's 90° to the door's edge. Use a square to align the hinge when inserting the screws.

12 | A baseboard can be installed after the cabinet is secured in place. If this cabinet is a stand-alone, you should inset the legs $3^1/_2$" on each side. If the cabinet is in a run, you have to inset only the outside units to secure the baseboard. Kickboard clips are attached to the baseboard. These metal clips slip on the leg shafts and hold the board securely. On stand-alone or end-of-run cabinets, where the end of the front kickboard is exposed, edge tape must be applied.

13 | Shelf supports and the shelf can be installed at this point to complete the cabinet.

DRAWER-OVER-DOOR FRAMELESS BASE CABINETS

Drawer-over-door frameless base cabinets are commonly used for sink bases and in instances when a drawer, as well as storage space behind doors, is required. It's a common style of kitchen cabinet that is often preferred over the standard full-door unit.

This cabinet is built following the same steps used to build a standard frameless base. The only added step is the installation of a second rail. This rail is installed below the top rail with

a 6" space between them. However, that's not a hard design rule, so any height drawer space is fine.

The rail is needed for the top edges of the doors, as they require support in the center of a two-door cabinet. The rail doesn't have to be installed in narrow, single-door cabinets because each side of the door closes on the cabinet edges.

The 6" space means the drawer box is 5" high, because it's 1" less in height than the space. The drawer face is normally 1" higher than the space and 1" wider. The combination of drawer face plus door heights, and the space between them, should equal the overall height of your full-height doors. If I use 30"-high doors, I install a 7"-high drawer face, a door below at $22^{15}/_{16}$" high, and a space between them of $^1/_{16}$" to match the full door height.

The drawer box is installed using the European bottom-mount drawer glides that were detailed in chapter nine. The drawer-glide runners are mounted to the drawer box and cabinet sides, so no other support is required.

END-OF-RUN FRAMELESS CABINETS

Any cabinet that will have its sides visible can be covered with a panel. Often a door is used as an end panel. Veneer is also an option, or a sheet material that has wood veneer on one face and melamine on the other.

If you use veneer particleboards or plywood, the ends don't have to be covered. But a hidden joinery system for those visible cabinet sides is required. The best joinery method in this situation is a biscuit joint.

DRAWER-BANK FRAMELESS BASE CABINETS

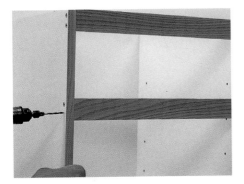

WOOD-STYLED FRAMELESS CABINETS

White melamine frameless cabinets can have wood surfaces and doors. In fact, this is a common application for large kitchen cabinet manufacturers.

Decide on the wood species you wish to use. Substitute melamine rails with hardwood in the base cabinets. Apply wood-veneer edge tape to the exposed cabinet edges and any exposed sides. Then use wood doors in place of the melamine doors. All visible surfaces will be covered with wood veneer and solid wood, but the cabinet interiors will be melamine.

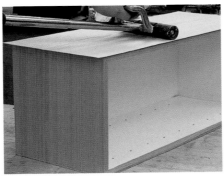

Wood veneer is available in large sheets with heat-activated glue. The sheets are pressed in place with an iron, rolled flat and then trimmed.

As mentioned previously, you may be able to find particleboard with both wood veneer and melamine faces on opposite sides. If not, veneer particleboard or plywood can also be used to build your frameless cabinets.

CALCULATING FRAMELESS DRAWER BOX & FACE HEIGHTS

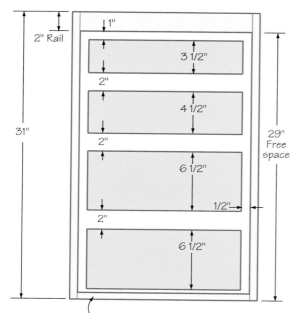

2" Rail

1"

3 1/2"

2"

4 1/2"

2"

31"

6 1/2"

1/2"

2"

6 1/2"

29"
Free
space

3/4"-(5/8"-) thick bottom board

- Cabinet door height is 30".

- Drawer box width is free space minus drawer box clearance on each side.

- 29" minus 8" = 21" for drawer boxes.

- Decide on size of drawer box heights = 21".

- Drawer faces are approximately 2" higher than the drawer height except top face which is total drawer face heights subtracted from door height in use.

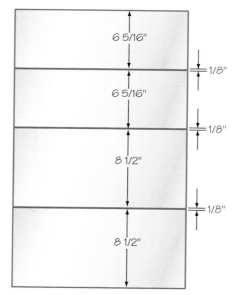

6 5/16"

1/8"

6 5/16"

1/8"

8 1/2"

1/8"

8 1/2"

TOP DRAWER FACE HEIGHT

- 30" -(8 1/2") - (8 1/2") - (6 1/2") = top drawer face height, less 1/8" space between drawer faces (or 6 1/8" in this example).

- Design choice; make top two drawer faces 6 5/16" high to balance look.

A drawer-bank base is constructed following the procedures for building a standard frameless base cabinet. These cabinets have only one top rail because the drawer faces rest against the cabinet side front edges. The drawer faces are spaced $\frac{1}{8}$" apart, and the total height of drawer faces and spaces should equal a full door height.

Follow the steps outlined in the technical drawing when building a

three- or four-drawer base cabinet. The free space is measured from the bottom edge of the top rail to the lower face of the bottom board. Drawer boxes require 1" above and below for proper clearance, so subtract the necessary clearance total, depending on the number of drawer boxes you install, from the free space.

The usable drawer space can be divided into three or four drawer boxes of

any size. You can follow the example in the drawing, use four $5\frac{1}{2}$" drawer boxes for that usable space, or decide on any combination of sizes you require.

The two or three bottom drawer faces in the case of a three-drawer cabinet, are 2" higher than the drawer boxes. The top face is the sum of all lower faces plus spaces between, subtracted from a total door height, which in this example is 30".

CUTTING LIST FOR A 36" (914MM) CORNER BASE CABINET USING ⅝" (16MM) THICK SHEET MATERIAL

inches (millimeters)

REFERENCE	QUANTITY	PART	STOCK	THICKNESS	(mm)	WIDTH	(mm)	LENGTH	(mm)	COMMENTS
A	2	sides	melamine pb	⅝	(16)	23³⁄₈	(594)	31	(787)	
B	1	bottom	melamine pb	⅝	(16)	34³⁄₄	(883)	34³⁄₄	(883)	cut as illustrated in drawing
C	2	backs	melamine pb	⅝	(16)	23³⁄₈	(594)	31	(787)	
D	1	back	melamine pb	⅝	(16)	18	(457)	31	(787)	cut oversize, then sides are angle-cut at 45° to fit
E	2	doors	melamine pb	⅝	(16)	11	(279)	30-high	(762)	
F	1	rail	melamine pb	⅝	(16)	2	(51)	12	(305)	
G	1	rail	melamine pb	⅝	(16)	2	(51)	11³⁄₈	(289)	

BUILDING A 36" FRAMELESS CORNER LAZY SUSAN BASE

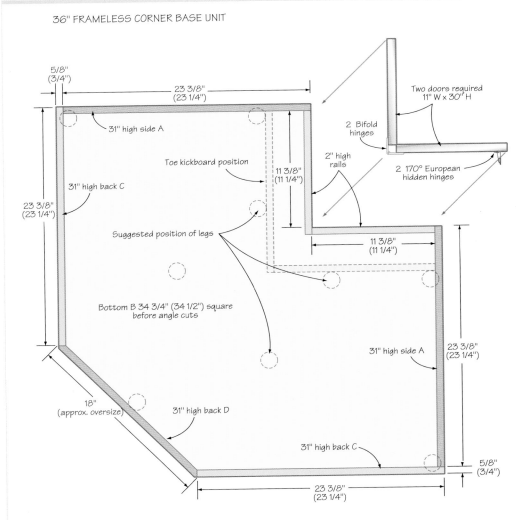

36" FRAMELESS CORNER BASE UNIT

5/8"
(3/4")

23 3/8"
(23 1/4")

31" high side A

Toe kickboard position

31" high back C

23 3/8"
(23 1/4")

Suggested position of legs

Bottom B 34 3/4" (34 1/2") square
before angle cuts

18"
(approx. oversize)

31" high back D

11 3/8"
(11 1/4")

2" high rails

11 3/8"
(11 1/4")

31" high side A

23 3/8"
(23 1/4")

31" high back C

5/8"
(3/4")

23 3/8"
(23 1/4")

Two doors required
11" W x 30" H

2 Bifold hinges

2 170° European hidden hinges

* Lazy Susan mounts in center of base and is supported on top
by a cross brace attached by PB screws to the sides.

* 3/4" thick material dimensions in parentheses

The 36" corner lazy Susan cabinet makes excellent use of corner spaces in a kitchen. In many new homes, the corner cabinets are dead-ended (called blind corners), and the space is wasted. This is a great way to recover and utilize corner space in your kitchen. This cabinet is usually fitted with a 32" pie-cut lazy Susan assembly.

The 36" corner base is a large cabinet, and a little more difficult to build when compared to a standard frameless model. However, follow the steps and your corner base will be perfect.

CUTTING LIST FOR A 36" (914MM) CORNER BASE CABINET USING $^3/_4$" (19MM) THICK SHEET MATERIAL

inches (millimeters)

REFERENCE	QUANTITY	PART	STOCK	THICKNESS	(mm)	WIDTH	(mm)	LENGTH	(mm)	COMMENTS
A	2	sides	melamine pb	$^3/_4$	(19)	23$^1/_4$	(590)	31	(787)	
B	1	bottom	melamine pb	$^3/_4$	(19)	34$^1/_2$	(877)	34$^1/_2$	(877)	cut as illustrated in drawing
C	2	backs	melamine pb	$^3/_4$	(19)	23$^1/_4$	(590)	31	(787)	
D	1	back	melamine pb	$^3/_4$	(19)	18	(457)	31	(787)	cut oversize, then sides are angle-cut at 45° to fit
E	2	doors	melamine pb	$^3/_4$	(19)	11	(279)	30-high	(762)	
F	1	rail	melamine pb	$^3/_4$	(19)	2	(51)	12	(305)	
G	1	rail	melamine pb	$^3/_4$	(19)	2	(51)	11$^1/_4$	(285)	

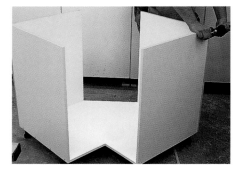

1 The cabinet has six PB pieces as indicated in the drawing and in the cutting lists. Cut the pieces as detailed. Do not cut the angles on the 18" by 31" backboard D at this time. I recommend that you cut it with straight cuts to the stated 18" by 31" size. Draw the front notch cutout lines and back angle cut line on the bottom B. Use a table saw to cut the two front notch lines, pushing the board in until the blade is about 3" away from the corner of the notch. The bottom of your blade will undercut farther into the board and will weaken the cutout. Follow the same procedures for the other line. Use a handsaw or jigsaw to complete the notch cutout. Next, guide the two front corners of the cutout section against the table saw fence with the fence set to a width of cut that will travel the blade along the angled back cut line. Be sure that your fence is long enough so that both cutout corners are tight against the fence for the full angled cut.

2 Apply iron-on edge tape to the notch cuts, then install the cabinet legs in the positions as indicated in the drawing. Maintain the 3$^1/_2$" setback from the front edges of the cabinet. Remember that this setback is required for kickboard spacing on all the base cabinets. Position the other legs so they will extend out from the edge of the bottom board by $^5/_8$" to aid in supporting the cabinet sides.

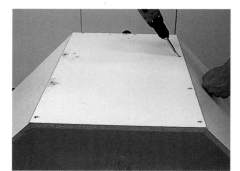

3 The front edges of the sides require edge tape before you start putting the cabinet panels together. Assemble the cabinet boards as shown, leaving the 18" by 31" backboard D until all others are secured. Use 2" PB screws in pilot holes, spaced every 8" on each panel. As well as securing the backs and sides to the bottom board, you'll also have to secure the backs to the sides with screws at each corner.

4 Measure the opening for the backboard D and fit it to the cabinet by cutting 45° angles on each side. It may be helpful the first time you build one of these cabinets to angle-cut the backboard so that it's a little larger, and trial fit the panel. Continue cutting the backboard slightly smaller after each trial fit until it's perfect.

Use 2" PB screws to attach the angled back to the bottom and backboards. Carefully site the screw line through the angled back and into the edge of the backs when drilling a pilot hole. It's a little difficult to drive screws at an angle, but take your time and drill the pilot hole accurately. Three screws on each side of the panel and two into the bottom board will hold it securely.

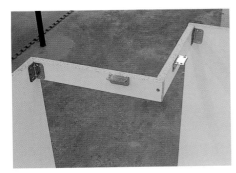

5 Cut both rails to the correct size and apply iron-on tape to the bottom edges. Secure the ends of each rail flush with the top edge of each cabinet side board using one 2"-long screw in the middle. Install right-angle brackets behind the rail to side board joints with $^5/_8$"-long screws. Drive one 2" screw centered on the edge, 1" from the top of each rail, at the intersection of both rails.

The rail system is very weak at this point, so be careful not to lift on either rail. Once right-angle brackets are installed and both rails are secured to the underside of the countertop they will be well supported and secure.

6 Install the angle clips, two per panel, so the countertop can be secured.

7 A board must be installed across the center of the cabinet to support the lazy Susan bearing assembly. This upper support is nothing more than a 4"-wide piece of $^5/_8$"- or $^3/_4$"-thick melamine particleboard that's the same length as the baseboard. Secure it with two 2"-long screws through the cabinet side boards. If you have difficulty locating this board, wait until you're ready to install the lazy Susan upper bearing support and locate it directly over the bearing.

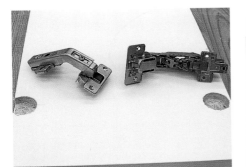

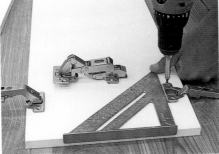

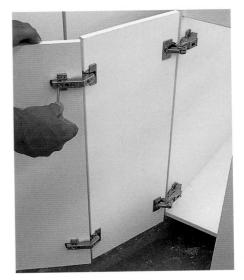

8 The door sizes on this cabinet are special. The 1"-plus rule doesn't apply here, so we use a calculation of notch length minus $^1/_4$" (for $^3/_4$"-thick material) or minus $^3/_8$" (for $^5/_8$"-thick material) for the doors. These two doors will have special hinges. First, drill 35mm-diameter holes in one door, following the standard steps for hinge hole positioning. These cabinet doors require 170° hinges, but they cannot be installed with a $^1/_8$"-thick spacer. The wide-opening hinge plates are properly aligned on the cabinet sides by temporarily installing a standard 100° to 120° hinge on the doors.

9 One of the two doors that have 35mm-diameter holes for the wide hinges will also need hinge holes drilled on the opposite edge of the door for bifold hinges. These special hinges secure the two doors to each other. The holes for the bifold-type hinges are drilled so the center of the 35mm hole is 12.5mm from the door's edge. That position will create a $^3/_4$" hole in the door, which is required for these hinges.

10 Follow the hinge and door mounting steps using the standard-opening hinge. Once the plates are properly located, switch the standard-opening hinges with the 170°-wide hinges. They will be attached to the hinge plates already mounted on the cabinet sides.

The bifold hinges that join both doors are installed following the directions supplied by the manufacturer. After installing the doors, follow the installation directions supplied with the lazy Susan assembly. Make sure it's properly positioned so the hinges don't run against the revolving shelves or affect door operation. The cabinet is now ready to be installed.

FINISHING CABINETS

TIPS, TECHNIQUES & MATERIALS

The most important step prior to finishing the wood is to prepare it by sanding and cleaning. Sanding removes any of the power tool marks that occur during the planing and dressing stages of cutting lumber. As well, you may discover dents or gouges in your hardwoods that require repairing. Fill minor abrasions with one of the many wood fillers on the market and prepare the wood as instructed on the container. If the gouge is serious, I'd consider replacing the piece, as it may be more trouble to try to repair the damage. For most filling, such as nail holes and very small gouges, I use a colored wax filler that will match the final finish.

Begin sanding with a course paper, such as 100-grit, then move up to 150-grit and finish sanding with 180- or 220-grit paper. I use the 100- and 150-grit papers on a random-orbit sander for most of my work, as it leaves few sanding marks and can be moved in any direction. The final sanding is done by hand with 180-grit paper.

Remember to be careful with glue on the joints, as it blocks the finish from penetrating into the wood and can leave a noticeable mark. It's best to wipe up the glue with a dry rag while it's still wet.

Many finishes are available on the market. They include paint and stains in any color imaginable, washed stains, polyurethane, oils and varnishes. Most finishing products are easy to apply and produce excellent results. However, check sample finishes on the type of wood you'll be using for your cabinets, and research all the properties. Check specifically for the product's hardness, resistance to stains from oils and grease, and its life expectancy. The finish will be subjected to a good deal of abuse in the kitchen from heat, moisture and handling.

The Internet is a good place to start your research on finishing products and techniques. Many major suppliers have information-based sites that are helpful. Some sites, such as the one run by the Hardwood Council at www.hardwoodcouncil.com, have on-line data and information brochures that you can order.

USING CLEAR NATURAL FINISHES

In the last few years about 80 percent of my kitchen cabinets have been finished with clear satin or semigloss oil-based polyurethane. The majority of clients seem to prefer the naturally finished wood cabinet. I have also finished a few kitchen projects using the semi-transparent washed stains that are easy to apply and produce excellent results.

Large cabinet shops often use lacquer finishes on their cabinet work. They apply the lacquer in spray booths with a paint compressor. These produce an excellent finish that dries quickly, allowing a two- or three-coat application over a short time period. The spray booth method requires a large space with special ventilation and is beyond the means and space availability of most woodworkers. Some shops specialize in finishing and you may want to use their services, if one is locally available.

Wood finishing is an art that takes practice and experience. I have tried many finishes and methods over the years, only to realize that there is much to learn in this field. I have taken finishing courses and read books on the subject. Good sources of information can be found in woodworking magazines. You will find numerous finishing manuals for sale, as well as many excellent articles on specific finishing techniques in these magazines.

APPLYING POLYURETHANE

As earlier stated, my preference over the last few years has been to apply oil-based polyurethane. I normally apply three coats with a good-quality brush, the first coat being thinned slightly, then I sand with 220-grit paper between each coat. The clear satin polyurethane produces a hard finish that doesn't readily show grease or fingerprints and is relatively easy to use.

Pollution and safety concerns have led to a move toward the safer, more environmentally friendly water-based stains and polyurethane. Latex polyurethane, one of these newer finishes, is water-based, quick drying and gives off little odor. However, I find that some water-based finishes tend to raise the grain, as water will do on wood, and produce a slightly cloudy finish. Other cabinet-makers I have spoken with use nothing but water-based finishes, which shows that the use of different finishing techniques and materials is a personal choice. Finishing is critical to the final product, particularly with wood cabinets. I would suggest you start with the oil- or water-based polyurethane and learn as much as possible about other products on the market. Document the finish used on each project because you might have to duplicate the results when building additional cabinets.

The best advice that I can give is to test three or four finishes on samples of the wood you want to use. Evaluate the results by view-ing the test pieces in the room where the cabinets will be installed. The extra effort is worthwhile as it's difficult to change an applied finish once the project has been completed.

MATERIALS LISTS AND CUTTING PLANS

THE FLOOR PLAN

A floor plan of the kitchen you are about to build is an important first step. It's your information source and road map to completing the project successfully. Draw the plan to scale so that any potential problems can be discovered before you begin construction. You'll find this exercise is valuable and the time spent will be well worth your effort.

Design software programs are available on the market for those of you who are familiar with computers. These programs, costing under $100, sometimes allow you to render a three-dimensional image of the proposed kitchen on the screen. A few programs allow you to move around in the kitchen, showing different perspectives of the cabinets.

However, the most important exercise is drawing a simple, scaled overhead floor plan like the example illustrated in the drawing on the following page. Accurately measure the room dimensions, locating all the doors, windows and any special features of the walls. You may have a plumbing run or heating duct pipe that has been boxed in with drywall that creates a bump-out on the wall. These special features have to be accounted for, as they may change your cabinet installation procedures.

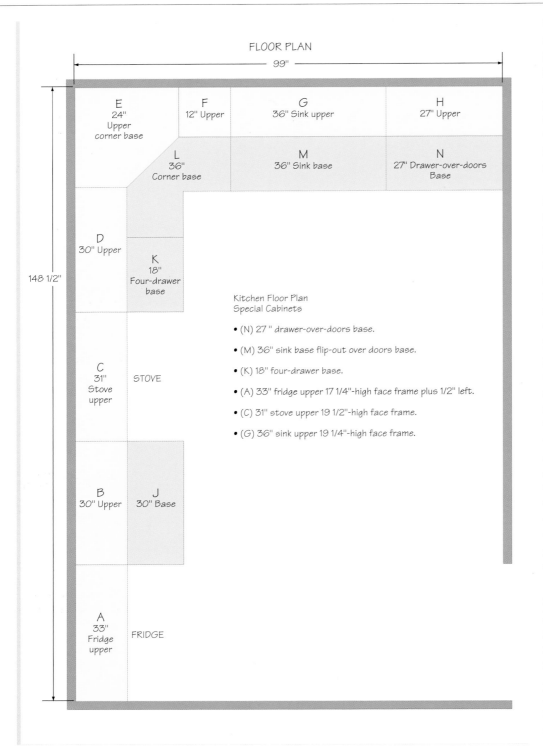

FLOOR PLAN
99"

| E | F | G | H |
| 24" Upper corner base | 12" Upper | 36" Sink upper | 27" Upper |

| L | M | N |
| 36" Corner base | 36" Sink base | 27" Drawer-over-doors Base |

148 1/2"

D
30" Upper

K
18"
Four-drawer
base

Kitchen Floor Plan
Special Cabinets

• (N) 27 " drawer-over-doors base.

• (M) 36" sink base flip-out over doors base.

• (K) 18" four-drawer base.

• (A) 33" fridge upper 17 1/4"-high face frame plus 1/2" left.

• (C) 31" stove upper 19 1/2"-high face frame.

• (G) 36" sink upper 19 1/4"-high face frame.

C
31"
Stove
upper

STOVE

B
30" Upper

J
30" Base

A
33"
Fridge
upper

FRIDGE

Use graph paper to scale the cabinets on your plan, so you get an accurate representation of the size and location of each unit. Analyze the plan, checking work triangle distances, traffic patterns, as well as the direction of opening for the cabinet doors, refrigerator and microwave.

The ideal floor plan is difficult to achieve given the dimensions of many kitchens. For example, the floor plan in the drawing above places the refrigerator at one end of the room and the sink on another wall at the other end of the room. The distance is greater than it should be for comfortable food preparation, but because of power requirements and the location of other appliances, we were forced to compromise. As well, a table cannot be placed in the center of the room, as it will seriously affect traffic patterns. In this case, a kitchen table was placed against the wall opposite the stove. It was the best alternative to many possible floor plans that were analyzed.

This floor plan is shown to illustrate that you sometimes have to work in existing rooms that do not allow us to follow all the accepted normal design practices. It's not an uncommon situation, and I'm sure some of you will be faced with design challenges such as this.

One alternative would be a complete relocation of existing services. This project was a kitchen in an old three-level apartment building, and budget constraints and tenants did not allow changes to existing services.

CREATING A MATERIALS LIST

Once the floor plan is finalized, create a materials cutting list. This list will allow you to calculate how much material to order, and provide you with a system to number each cut piece. An average kitchen requires one hundred or more PB pieces, so this list is invaluable during the assembly phase of your project.

The following table details a portion of the $^5/_8$" white melamine particleboard material cutting sizes that are required for the kitchen shown in the floor plan. Only two cabinets are shown to illustrate the process; in the full list, however, all the cabinets should be listed and part numbers assigned to each piece. It's a good way to identify each panel for your project; otherwise, you'll be measuring hundreds of times, trying to locate the proper panels for each cabinet.

If your cabinets are wood face-frame style, your cutting list should include those parts. Once again, these cutting lists may seem time-consuming, but they'll save you many hours and greatly lessen the frustration of trying to manage hundreds of panels and solid-wood parts.

MELAMINE PARTICLEBOARD CUTTING LIST FOR $^5/_8$" (16MM) THICK PB

inches (millimeters)

CABINET STYLE AND IDENTIFIER	CUT SIZE REQUIRED		PANEL REFERENCE NUMBER
A - 33" (838) fridge upper	2 sides @ $10^5/_8 \times 16^1/_2$	(270×419)	1, 2
**(17$^1/_4$" (438) high face	1 bottom @ $10^5/_8 \times 31^1/_{16}$	(270×789)	3
*plus $^1/_2$" (6) left	1 top @ $10^5/_8 \times 31^1/_{16}$	(270×789)	4
	1 back @ $32^7/_{16} \times 16^1/_2$	(824×419)	5
	1 shelf @ $10^5/_8 \times 31$	(270×787)	6
B - 30" standard face-frame upper	2 sides @ $10^5/_8 \times 31$	(270×787)	7, 8
	1 bottom @ $10^5/_8 \times 28^1/_{16}$	(270×713)	9
	1 top @ $10^5/_8 \times 28^1/_{16}$	(270×713)	10
	1 back @ $29^7/_{16} \times 31$	(748×787)	11
	2 shelves @ $10^5/_8 \times 28$	(270×711)	12, 13

*The "$^1/_2$" (6) left" reference means the left-side stile on this face-frame cabinet is $^1/_2$" (6mm) wider than normal. This cabinet needs to be scribed to a wall that isn't plumb or smooth. The cabinet is considered to be a 33"-wide (838mm) reduced-height upper with a $^1/_2$" (6mm) scribe left. The cabinet panel sizes don't change, as they are considered to be for a 33"-wide (838mm) cabinet; only the face-frame stile width changes.

**Notice that the face-frame height is $^3/_4$" (19mm) longer than the cabinet side. That rule applies to all face-frame cabinets.

$^3/_4$" (19MM) THICK WOOD FACE FRAME CUTTING LIST

inches (millimeters)

CABINET STYLE AND IDENTIFIER	CUT SIZE REQUIRED		FRAME PART REFERENCE NUMBER
A - 33" (838) fridge upper (17$^1/_4$" (438) high face frame) plus $^1/_2$" (6) left	1 stile left @ $1^1/_2 \times 17^1/_4$	(38×438)	1
	1 stile right @ $1 \times 17^1/_4$	(25×438)	2
	2 rails @ $1^1/_2 \times 31$	(38×787)	3, 4
B - 30" (762) standard upper	2 stiles @ $1 \times 31^3/_4$	(25×806)	5, 6
	2 rails @ $1^1/_2 \times 28$	(38×711)	7, 8

Wood face-frame or frameless cabinets also need a list of door and drawer sizes. You can create a parts list off this one if you plan to build your own drawers. If you are going to purchase doors, this list will be required by the supplier.

CABINET DOOR AND DRAWER FACE LIST

inches (millimeters)

CABINET STYLE AND IDENTIFIER	DOOR AND/OR DRAWER SIZE		QUANTITY
A - 33" (838) fridge upper (17$^1/_4$" (438) high face frame) plus $^1/_2$" (6) left	16-wide $\times$ 16-high door	(406-wide $\times$ 406-high door)	2
B - 30" (787) standard upper	14$^1/_2$-wide $\times$ 30$^1/_2$-high door	(369-wide $\times$ 775-high door)	2

Preparing the cutting lists should take you one to two hours, depending on the complexity of the kitchen design. However, it will probably be the most effective two hours that you'll spend building the kitchen. These lists are critical, as they define the sizes of the finished pieces for the carcasses, face frames, doors and drawer faces.

I transfer the carcass cutting list sizes to a diagram of 4' × 8' sheet material. Sheets are drawn with the reference numbers relating to each individual piece. Once completed, this layout provides information on the number of pieces of 4' × 8' material you will require. This process also minimizes the waste that occurs because you can move pieces around to get the best results prior to cutting. The quantity of sheet goods required is also necessary when calculating your material cost.

Preparing the cutting lists and sheet layout diagrams reduces the amount of time required to cut the cabinet parts to size. Cutting the 4' × 8' material can be a tiring and time consuming process without proper planning.

CREATING A HARDWARE LIST

The hardware requirements should also be calculated during this planning and layout phase. It doesn't have to be precise to the last screw required, but it should be a fairly accurate representation of the hardware needed. Material ordering and cost can be calculated based on this list. The following is a typical hardware list, based on the example design.

HARDWARE REQUIREMENTS

ITEM DESCRIPTION	QUANTITY
2" (51mm) particleboard screws	500
5/8" (16mm) hinge & angle clip screws	200
cabinet legs	30
plinth clips for toe kickboards	12
countertop angle brackets	25
2" (51mm) spiral finishing nails	100
adjustable shelf pins	60
100° full-overlay hinge assemblies	38
170° full-overlay hinge assemblies	4
double door hinge assemblies for corner base cabinet	2
18"-dia. (457mm-dia.) full-round lazy Susan	1
32"-dia. (813mm-dia.) pie-cut lazy Susan	1
door and drawer handles	27
door bumpers	50
22" (559mm) European drawer glides	5
cut-to-fit cutlery tray for cabinet K	1
5/8" (16mm) plastic cap moulding for shelves	40 feet (3.6m)
door-mounted towel rack for base M	1

COUNTERTOP REQUIREMENTS

The countertop size should be calculated at this time. For our sample kitchen we will need a $30\frac{3}{4}$" run for cabinet J so we'll have $\frac{3}{8}$" overhang on each side. Both sides should have a $\frac{1}{4}$" veneer panel (no moulding is needed) beside the stove and fridge. The other countertop section required will be a right-angle joined section. The left-side run will be $54\frac{3}{8}$" long (this dimension includes the $\frac{3}{8}$" overhang on the left side of cabinet K), and the right leg will be 99" long with an unfinished end.

If you are building a custom wood-edged countertop as detailed in chapter eight, you will have to order the PB, 1×2 hardwood edge, 1×3 wood for the backsplash and laminate. If it's to be a standard roll countertop from a local supplier, send your order in, as there can be a delay if the chosen design is not locally stocked. This issue of stock countertop designs should be discussed with your supplier to avoid delays, as some designs can take four to six weeks to arrive from the manufacturer.

ADDITIONAL MATERIAL REQUIREMENTS

Material required for finishing should also be calculated at this stage, including: $\frac{1}{4}$" veneer-covered plywood for finishing the exposed sides of cabinet J, the left side of cabinet K, and half the exposed sides of cabinets B, D, F and H (this veneer plywood is also required to cover the underside of the upper cabinets); 1×4 hardwood for the kickboards; and top moulding for the upper cabinets.

CREATING A PROJECT FILE

I create a working file for each project. In it I include my notes on the various designs and changes, the final layout, my cutting lists, order lists and any other information relating to this project. As the project proceeds I will add information on ordering, the hardware style numbers and final comments after the project is completed.

I find the file system to be one of my most valuable tools. I can refer to the project at any time and use the information in the future. You may run into a situation where you need an extra door handle, or a replacement door, or you may want to add another section two or three years down the road; it's a real plus to have all the information on file. If you don't have a great memory, the project file is an invaluable tool.

PROJECT PLANNING

I lay out all my needs on the cutting lists, order the materials, get firm delivery commitments from any subcontractors such as my countertop supplier or cabinet door supplier, and calculate shop time needed to build the cabinets. I can then realistically plan when to tear out the old cabinets and install the new kitchen. This gives you the opportunity to arrange for the other required services, such as new flooring installation, new appliance delivery, the plumber or possibly an electrician. You can also start making plans for kitchen downtime and all the lifestyle changes for your family.

The planning stage is critical. A project can turn into a real nightmare if you make mistakes at this point in the process. I'm not suggesting that this is a difficult process; it's actually very simple, but unfortunately many people do not pay enough attention to this stage and get into serious trouble. Analyze all the required steps, detail your material needs, estimate realistic time frames based on the data, and keep the other people who you will have to depend on informed about your progress.

SHOP ASSEMBLY PROCEDURES

SOME HELPFUL HOW-TO'S

1 | If you are building the face-frame version, cut to size and assemble the hardwood face frames so they can be sanded and finished. For this particular kitchen project I finished the face frames with three coats of clear satin polyurethane. Do not finish the back side of the face frame, as it will be glued to the carcass edge.

You will be able to start assembling the carcasses while finishing the face frames and doors. You can also calculate how many, as well as the sizes of, end panels and undercabinet ¼" veneer plywood panels required. They can be cut and finished along with the face frames and doors.

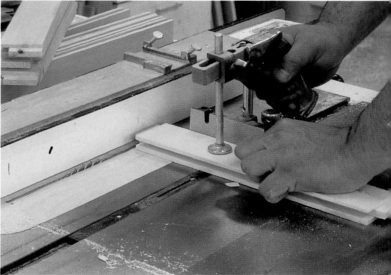

2 | Assemble and finish doors and drawer faces with the face frames while cutting and assembling the carcass.

3 Rip 4' × 8' sheets of sheet material to size with the aid of the cutting lists and layout sheets. Melamine-coated particleboard edges chip easily, so take special precautions. Primarily, equip your table saw with a carbide-tipped melamine PB blade. Melamine PB has a tendency to chip on one side more than the other. I orient the boards during cutting so the good side is always maintained.

The only boards that will be exposed on both sides are the shelf boards and the drawer carcass sides. Chipping can be minimized on these boards by double-cutting: Set the saw blade at half the thickness of the melamine PB and cut on one side, then flip the PB over to complete the cut on the other side.

4 Following the ripping step, crosscut the boards on a radial-arm or table saw. If the boards are extra wide, such as in the case of the base cabinet boards, I use a sliding table attachment on my table saw, or you can just as easily use a circular saw and straightedge. Since the saw chips on one side more than the other, always pay attention to the board's good side when you orient it. Mark each piece with its reference number.

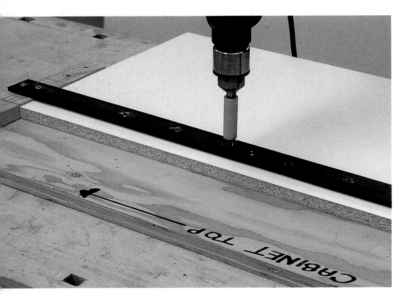

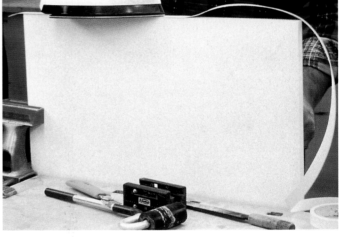

6 If you are building the frameless cabinet version, apply edge tape to all edges that will be visible after the cabinet is installed. Use wood veneer or white melamine edge tape to match the cabinet doors.

5 Verify the board sizes, then begin the assembly of the cabinets. First, drill the upper cabinet sides for the adjustable shelf pins.

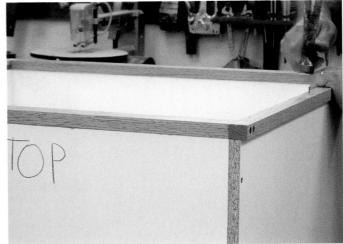

7 Now fasten the sides to the top and bottom boards with 2" particle-board screws. Install the back flush with the bottom and top board, as well as one side board.

When using the 2" PB screws, make certain to drill a ⅛" pilot hole through the board to be secured, and into the center of the edge of the second board. Use a marking gauge set at ⁵⁄₁₆" for ⅝" material and ⅜" for ¾" stock as a guide for the drill bit. The screws should be tight; however, be careful they are not overtightened. I use a ⅛" drill bit in a carbide-tipped ⅜" countersunk assembly to a depth that allows the screw head to be set flush with the surface of the PB.

8 Install the face frame on the cabinet, making sure of the orientation of any special face frames. For example, if cabinet A has a 1½" stile on the left side, designated on the drawing as + ½" L, the face frame must be installed with respect to that orientation. Set the face-frame outside top flush with the carcass outside top. The carcass edges should be hidden, and then glue and nail the face frame to the carcass as previously described.

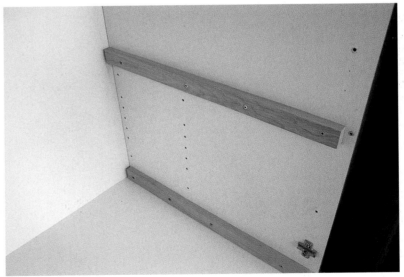

10 The first step in assembling the base cabinets is determining whether the cabinet will have a shelf or pullout installed. Drill holes for the shelf pins or fasten the wood cleats at the correct height, with 1¼" screws in pilot holes, through the outside of the cabinet side into the cleat.

9 Cut the plastic cap moulding to fit the exposed edge of the shelves and secure with contact cement or a glue gun. The cap moulding fits tightly on the ⅝" melamine; however, I add a little glue to make sure it's held firmly in place.

11 Fasten the sides to the bottom board and install the backboard. When installing the backboard, verify that the inside dimension of the cabinet is correct at the top of the cabinet, between the two sides. The base cabinet does not require a top board; however, you must make sure the inside dimension, at the top, is correct, to guarantee a square and plumb cabinet.

The top edge of the backboard must be aligned with the top edges of the sides so the countertop will sit flat on the cabinet. If you are building the frameless version, install the upper rail as detailed in chapter ten.

13 Install the countertop brackets with $^5/_8$" screws. Use two brackets per panel on the back of the top rail, making sure they are flush with the top edges of the cabinet.

12 Install the cabinet legs, four on cabinets under 30" wide and six on cabinets over 30" wide, on the base's bottom board. Install the legs so that they extend out from the baseboard by $^5/_8$" to help support the sides. The exception is when the cabinet is an open-ended cabinet and the kickboard has to be recessed $3^1/_2$" from the cabinet edge. Install the cabinet legs so that they are $3^1/_2$" back from the face edge of the bottom board.

14 Install the face frame as previously described, noting any special orientation. Check that the top of the face frame is flush with the top of the sides and that the side overlaps are equal.

15 At this point, cut to size and apply $^1/_4$" plywood veneer to any cabinet side that will be visible. In the sample layout in chapter twelve, veneer plywood will be attached with contact cement to the right and left side of cabinet J, the left side of cabinet K, the right and left side of cabinet B, the left side of cabinet D, the right side of cabinet F and the left side of cabinet H. On the upper cabinets, extend the veneer plywood below the side so that it will cover the end of the veneer plywood that will be applied to the underside of the upper cabinets. If you want to add wood doorstop moulding as a perimeter trim with standard 1"-wide stiles, you must use a thinner veneer. Apply a $^1/_8$"-thick, or less, veneer to the cabinet sides so that you can use the $^1/_4$"-thick wood doorstop moulding.

16 Assemble the drawers, as previously detailed in chapter nine, and check the operation. Follow the drawer glide manufacturer's instructions with respect to clearances. Drawer side clearances are critical, so try to be as accurate as possible with your cutting and assembly procedures.

17 Drill the doors with a 35mm flat-bottom drill bit at 3" or 4" centers from the top and bottom of the door, and $\frac{1}{8}$" in from the door edge. Pay particular attention to the door orientation if the door is designed with a top and bottom. Some door styles can be reversed while other designs, such as a cathedral style, must be installed one way. In some instances you have a right and left door. With single-door cabinets, the side you want the door to open on will determine where the holes are drilled. Mount the doors on the cabinets as previously described in chapter nine.

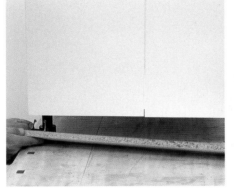

18 Drill the holes in the drawer faces for the handles you will be installing. Position the drawer faces on the cabinet with the drawer box in place. Drive screws through the handle holes, into the drawer box, to temporarily secure the face. Open the drawer, with face attached, and drive $1\frac{1}{4}$" screws through the back of the drawer box front board and into the back of the drawer face.

Remove the temporary screws and drill holes through the drawer box, using the drawer face holes as a guide, and then install the handles.

19 Leave the kickboards longer than required to allow custom fitting during installation. Test fit a sample section to verify correct leg placement and kickboard height.

20 Order your countertops if you plan to use the standard roll style for your kitchen project. If you're making the wood-edged top, follow the steps in chapter eight.

This completes the assembly process and the cabinets are ready to be installed. Compare the cabinets, noting any special features such as drawers, pullouts, wider stiles and door opening direction, with the layout to guarantee that all dimensions and requirements are correct.

EXISTING CABINET TEAR-OUT

Unless you're building cabinets for a new home, you'll be faced with tearing out the existing kitchen cabinets. And unless they are reasonably modern cabinets, you'll most likely find they were built in place.

Carpenter or stick built-in-place cabinets depend heavily on the structural support from existing walls. Therefore, finding fastening devices such as screws and nails can sometimes be quite a challenge. I've seen every fastening device under the sun when tearing out existing cabinets. It can be fun to see various support systems that have been installed.

Be careful and take your time tearing out old cabinets. Electrical wiring is often hidden, plumbing is sometimes routed through cabinets, and heating ducts may have been directed under the existing base cabinets.

In the interest of safety, I suggest you turn off the water supply and electrical service to the kitchen area, as well as other nearby rooms. This safety measure will help avoid accidents or damage should you inadvertently break a water line or cut a power cable.

CABINET INSTALLATION

Support the upper cabinets with blocks or a strong wooden box prior to removing screws or nails. The sudden weight shift downward when the last fastener is removed can be surprising. Always, if possible, enlist the help of someone to stabilize the cabinet as you remove the fasteners. Again, with respect to upper cabinets, remove all loose assemblies, such as shelves, to lighten them. You'll also avoid the danger of having shelving fall on you should the cabinet suddenly tip. I remove the cabinet doors before taking the fasteners out to further lighten the load.

Removing base cabinets can be hazardous even though they appear to be sitting on the floor. Rotten floor support systems or poorly connected kick platforms may cause the base cabinet to fall forward when the last screw is removed. Again, enlist the aid of another person to support the assembly when removing fastening devices.

SITE PREPARATION

Site preparation prior to new cabinet installation is an important process. Verify that water and waste supply lines are in the correct location, and that electrical service is sufficient and correctly positioned. If you plan to move the sink location, now is an excellent time to reroute supply lines. The frameless and face-frame cabinet building systems detailed in this book incorporate a full backboard on both upper and lower units. Therefore, you can remove wall sheathing to allow changes in supply line positioning.

The same is true with electrical service lines. Verify that outlets are in the correct location and at the correct height. Base cabinet height is 36", but you must also account for the height of the countertop backsplash, which can often add an additional 4" to the overall base height.

Use a long level or straightedge to check the wall condition. You'll never find a perfect wall, but a wall stud that has badly bowed over time can cause problems during new cabinet installation. If you find a bad bulge in any of the walls, remove the sheeting and correct the problem.

NEW CABINET INSTALLATION

Cabinet installation methods vary depending on the installer. The primary difference is whether to begin by installing the uppers or the bases. Each method has its merits, as there is no absolute correct way of installing cabinets. Find a process that you are comfortable with to achieve the end result: properly installed cabinets.

I will describe my method of cabinet installation based on our sample kitchen layout from chapter twelve.

THE STARTING POINT

You should be aware of some considerations before proceeding. Often a room is out of square and walls are not plumb. This can cause a number of problems during cabinet installation. In our sample kitchen, I will go through the process as described, checking the room dimensions for cabinet runs that are between walls. For example, referring to the drawing in chapter twelve, the N to L base cabinet run is between two walls, so verify that your space requirements are correct as you install each cabinet. It's possible for the wall at L to be out of plumb enough that your cabinet will not fit. Hold your level vertically on the wall to determine if the wall is out of plumb. It's best to test fit your cabinets prior to anchoring them permanently in place.

In our sample kitchen, the upper cabinet runs are both closed runs. This is typically the most difficult installation. In this situation I would start in the corner with cabinet E and work out to both sides, always checking my remaining distances to avoid any serious problems. It can be frustrating if you have to remove installed cabinets to plane a face frame because you've run out of space.

The first step in cabinet installation is to determine the level or slope of the floor and how much the walls are out f plumb. This is your biggest challenge when installing kitchen cabinets. When wall are out of plumb, adjustable cabinet legs allow for easier installation as compared to the constructed base support assembly system. And the overhang of the face frame allows room for scribing cabinets to an out-of-plumb wall.

Draw a level line on the walls around the room at a reference height of $35\frac{1}{4}$" from the floor. After drawing the line with a level, measure from the floor to the line at various positions around the room. Determine the highest point in the room. (It will be the place with the smallest distance from that level reference line to the floor.) Start your base cabinet installation from that high point, setting the top edge of the base at $35\frac{1}{4}$". That height, plus the thickness of the countertop material, will set the top surface at the required 36" above the floor.

All floors have a slope, some greater than others, and it's important that you determine the high point. If you start installing cabinets in an area other than the high point, you may not have sufficient adjustment range on the legs.

Locating the Wall Studs

1 Use a wall stud finder to locate the first and second stud.

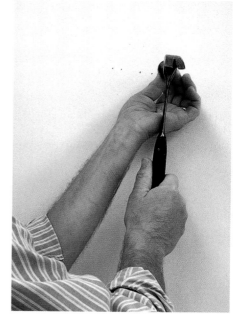

2 Drive a small finishing nail into the mark and locate the outer limits of the studs. Mark the centers of both studs.

4 Use a long level to extend the stud lines below the upper cabinet position and above the base cabinet tops.

3 Measure the distance between studs and mark the stud locations around the room. You may want to check the locations with your stud finder to satisfy yourself that the stud center-to-center distances are staying constant.

Installing the Cabinets

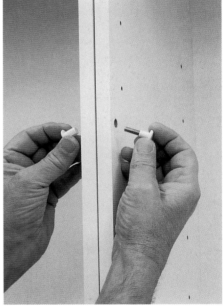

1 Install a base cabinet at the highest point in the room. If you cannot start at the highest point, be aware of the adjustment limits with the cabinet legs. Level that base cabinet and anchor it to the wall with 3" screws into the studs. Four screws per cabinet are more than enough to firmly secure the base units.

After the first cabinet has been installed, continue in either direction, leveling and securing the cabinets. The procedure changes slightly with the second cabinet. For frameless cabinetry, join the front edge of the second cabinet flush with the first cabinet's front edge and secure with 1" screws through the cabinet sides. When installing face-frame cabinets, join the stiles together and use 1¼" screws through the stiles. Now anchor the back of the cabinet to the wall.

2 When installing face-frame cabinets, remove the doors and clamp the left-side stile of one cabinet to the right-side stile of the adjacent cabinet. Be sure the face frames are flush with each other.

Drill a ⅛" countersunk pilot hole through one stile and partially into the other. Drill a hole slightly larger than the screw body thickness through the stile on the screw-head side to allow the screw to rotate freely in that stile to prevent bridging (the effect caused when the screw threads into both pieces of wood being fastened, preventing the pieces from being drawn tightly together). Fasten the stiles together with three 1¼" screws at the top, middle and bottom. Then anchor the cabinet to the wall with 3" screws through the backboard and into the wall studs.

3 The same procedure holds true for frameless cabinets, except they are tied together with 1" screws or double-headed bolts at the front edge.

4 | All cabinets, particularly the first upper and base, must be plumb. Use a long level to read the position, and shim the cabinet into plumb if necessary. A small fraction out of plumb will cause a great deal of trouble, particularly on long runs of cabinets.

5 | A level cabinet is equally important. Use a good level to properly locate the cabinet before it's permanently anchored to the wall.

6 | You may be required to scribe the stile if it isn't tight against the wall or the countertop to achieve a snug fit along the wall contours. Check the fit after leveling the cabinet and use a compass, adjusted to the widest part of the gap, between the wall and stile, as your reference. Holding the point of the compass against the wall, draw a pencil line on the stile face. Use a sharp plane and remove wood up to the pencil line until you get a tight fit. You may find that a belt sander does the job when you have many contours in the wall.

The same process holds true for countertop fitting. A countertop usually requires scribing and fitting as most walls are not perfectly flat. Draw the line and use a belt sander to remove material.

7 | Install the remainder of the base cabinets in the same manner. With respect to the sample layout, set the stile-to-stile spacing between cabinets K and J at 31". This will provide clearance for a $3/8$" countertop overhang on cabinet K and J and leave a $30^{1}/_{4}$" space for the stove.

8 | Install the countertop, scribing and removing material if necessary, so that the countertop fits tightly against the wall. Overhang the small countertop on base cabinet J by $3/8$" on each side. Use $3/8$" screws in the brackets to secure the countertop in place.

9 | Attach the upper cabinets to the wall with four 3" wood screws through the backboard into the wall studs. The first cabinet must be level and plumb, as it's the reference point for all the upper cabinets. Verify your remaining space after installing each cabinet. With regards to the sample kitchen in chapter twelve, cabinets A and H will probably require stile scribing to get a perfect fit.

Install the remainder of the upper cabinets, being sure they are well supported. Level the cabinets, screw the adjoining stiles to each other and anchor the cabinets to the wall. The bottoms of the stiles must be even on the cabinets. Reduced-height cabinets (cabinets G, C and A) should be installed with the cabinet tops in line with the top edges of the other upper cabinets.

10 Install veneer plywood on the underside of all upper cabinets with either contact cement or brad nails. I have also successfully used high-quality construction cement, which is much quicker to apply than contact cement.

11 Cut to size and install trim moulding on the top edge of the upper cabinets. Any errors in stile length cutting or gaps between the stiles can be left at the top of the cabinets and will be covered by the moulding. Trim moulding style is dependent on individual taste. I've installed everything from 1" bead to 4" crown moulding to achieve different finished appearances. Purchase short lengths of a number of moulding styles and experiment until you find a pleasing style.

INSTALLING APPLIANCES

Installing appliances is always challenging. Always verify your appliance dimensions before beginning the kitchen design process. One common point of frustration in the kitchen cabinetmaking industry is with ranges. Many cabinetmakers leave 31" of space between lower cabinets for range placement. This allowance provides for $\frac{3}{8}$" countertop overhang on each cabinet side and $\frac{1}{4}$" clearance between the countertop sides and the range for easy removal and replacement during cleaning. However, range hoods, which are installed above the range, are exactly 30" wide and look properly installed when there isn't any space on either side. The simplest way I've found to overcome the problem, and to have the upper and lower cabinets align, is to add $\frac{1}{2}$" to each upper cabinet stile on either side of the over-the-stove cabinet. The upper stove cabinet, being 30" wide, will allow installation of the range hood without space on each side. The added stile width (now a $1\frac{1}{2}$" stile), on each of the upper cabinets to the right and left of the upper stove cabinet, will force them in line with the lower cabinets. This added stile width is only on the upper cabinet's side that butts against the upper stove cabinet.

COMPLETING THE CABINET INSTALLATION

It's important that you avoid racking (twisting) the cabinet during installation. Most walls are not straight. Many have irregular surfaces and are not plumb. When anchoring cabinets to the wall, verify that the cabinet back is touching the wall, and if there is a gap, use a shim to fill the space. I find cedar shims work well because they are tapered. Always check the level, front to back and side to side, as well as the plumb of each cabinet before and after you anchor it securely.

Cut the kickboards to length, install the plinth clips and secure the boards to the cabinet legs. Use butt joints where the kickboards intersect at right angles. If the floor is out of level, you may have to scribe the bottom of the kickboard to get a tight fit. Alternatively, you can use quarter-round moulding, which is flexible, to fill the gaps between the floor and the kickboard. Simply nail the quarter-round to the kickboard while holding it tightly against the floor.

Install doorstop moulding around the perimeter on the exposed base and upper cabinet sides. Use mitered corners with the moulding to form a perimeter picture frame. This adds visual depth to the cabinet ends. As well, any wall irregularities can be hidden, as the moulding is slightly flexible and can be pushed into the contours of the wall. It's best to cut and install one moulding piece at a time to give you the tightest fit possible.

suppliers

ADAMS & KENNEDY – THE WOOD SOURCE
6178 Mitch Owen Road
P.O. Box 700
Manotick, Ontario K4M 1A6
613-822-6800
www.wood-source.com
Wood supply

DELTA MACHINERY
90 Passmore Lane
Jackson, Tennessee 38305
800-223-7278 (in US)
800-463-3582 (in Canada)
www.deltawoodworking.com
Woodworking tools

EXAKTOR WOODWORKING TOOLS, INC.
4 Glenbourne Park
Markham, Ontario L6C 1G9
800-387-9789
www.excal-tools.com
Accessories for the table saw

HOUSE OF TOOLS LTD.
100 Mayfield Common Northwest
Edmonton, Alberta T5P 4B3
780-944-9600
www.houseoftools.com
Woodworking tools and hardware

JESSEM TOOL COMPANY
171 Robert T. E. # 7 & # 8
Penetanguishene, Ontario L9M 1G9
800-436-6799
www.jessem.com
Rout-R-Slide and Rout-R-Lift

LEE VALLEY TOOLS LTD.

USA:
P.O. Box 1780
Ogdensberg, New York 13669-6780
800-267-8735

Canada:
P.O. Box 6295, Station J
Ottawa, Ontario K2A 1T4
800-267-8761
www.leevalley.com
Fine woodworking tools and hardware

PORTER CABLE
4825 Highway 45 North
P.O. Box 2468
Jackson, Tennessee 38302-2468
800-487-8665
www.porter-cable.com
Woodworking tools

RICHELIEU HARDWARE
7900 West Henri-Bourassa
Ville St. Laurent, Quebec H4S 1V4
800-619-5446 (in US)
800-361-6000 (in Canada)
www.richelieu.com
Hardware supplies

ROCKLER WOODWORKING AND HARDWARE
4365 Willow Drive
Medina, Minnesota 55340
800-279-4441
www.rockler.com
Woodworking tools and hardware

TENRYU AMERICA, INC.
7964 Kentucky Drive, Suite 12
Florence, Kentucky 41042
800-951-7297
www.tenryu.com
Saw blades

TOOL TREND LTD.
140 Snow Boulevard
Concord, Ontario L4K 4L1
416-663-8665
Woodworking tools and hardware

VAUGHAN & BUSHNELL MANUFACTURING
11414 Maple Avenue
Hebron, Illinois 60034
815-648-2446
www.vaughanmfg.com
Hammers and other tools

WOLFCRAFT NORTH AMERICA
1222 W. Ardmore Avenue
P.O. Box 687
Itasca, Illinois 60143
630-773-4777
www.wolfcraft.com
Woodworking hardware and accessories

WOODCRAFT
P.O. Box 1686
Parkersburg, West Virginia 26102-1686
800-225-1153
www.woodcraft.com
Woodworking hardware and accessories

index